25 —
INSCRIBED/SIGNED

To Linda,

Seize the
!

AF531045

Kay

12/21/14

TAKING THE BULL BY THE HORNS

Also by Ray E. Aquitania, M.D.

Jock-Docs:
World-Class Athletes
Wearing White Coats

TAKING THE BULL BY THE HORNS

RAY E. AQUITANIA, M.D.

Printed in the
United States of America

TAKING THE BULL BY THE HORNS
Copyright © 2013
Ray E. Aquitania, M.D.

First printing
Published by BookLocker.com
All Rights Reserved

Library of Congress Control Number: 2013903140
ISBN: 978-1-62646-306-6

All Rights Reserved. No part of this publication may be reproduced, stored in a retrieval system, or transmitted in any form or by any means, electronic, mechanical, photocopying, recording, or otherwise, without written permission of the publisher. Thank you for your support of the author's rights.

This work is a memoir. Events, actions, and experiences and their consequences over a period of years have been retold as the author presently recollects them. Out of an abundance of respect for individuals' privacy, the names and identifying characteristics of certain individuals in this book have been changed. In addition, some dialogue has been recreated from memory.

For Sienna

If everything seems
under control,
you're just not going
fast enough

--- Mario Andretti

The Contents

TAKING THE BULL BY THE HORNS

Prologue

"I wonder if anyone has thought about what would happen if someone actually attempted to do this. It definitely wouldn't be pretty. First of all, it's highly unlikely that someone would be able to grab the horns in the first place, because they're attached to two tons of hooves, muscle, and anger management problems."

So wrote Aaron Rimstidt in *The Saturday Evening Post* in the spring of 2012. This frequent *Post* contributor was commenting on the cliché "take the bull by the horns" with some tongue-in-cheek humor.

Some contend that this famous phrase actually stems from astrology. Taurus, the bull, has a reputation for trouble and boisterous activity. So if you grab the horns of this unruly beast and bring him under control, you are dealing forcefully and directly with a challenging situation.

But according to Robert Hendrickson in his book *The Facts on File Encyclopedia of Word and Phrase Origins*, this expression can be traced back to bullfighting. In that pastime, he relates that "Spanish *banderilleros* plant darts in the neck of the bull and tire him more by waving cloaks and seizing him by the horns, trying to hold his head down."

Alternatively, Hendrickson thinks the idiom could have originated in North America, where "rawboned early ranchers in the American Southwest also wrestled bulls or steers in a popular sport called *bulldogging* (also called *steer wrestling*) that is still seen in rodeos."

Today, the business world is one major arena in which this saying is widely expressed. Case in point: In her book *Take the Bull by the Horns*, Gayle Lantz, a successful leadership development consultant, promotes strategies to help people achieve what they want in their careers by facing problems directly.

Unlike Lantz, I look at this idiom beyond the business and professional worlds. To me, when one is away from the office setting, the phrase "taking the bull by the horns" signifies taking the initiative in confronting difficult or uncertain situations not related to work. With this attitude, a person can face up to challenges and diverse problems in a direct and determined way.

Intimately related to the above concept is the ability to make the most of each day. As the Roman lyric poet Horace wrote in his Odes Book 1 in 23 B.C., *"Carpe diem, quam minimum credula postero."* In other words, "Pluck (seize) the day, putting as little trust as possible in tomorrow."

Of course, it is never as simple as saying that we should live in the moment and disregard all consequences. If that were the case, there would be no need for financial planning and medical insurance. Nonetheless, the philosophy of Horace has motivated many to realize the importance of the present.

There is seldom a day that goes by that I don't embrace the ideas of taking the bull by the horns and *carpe diem* (seize the day). With these tools, I have addressed many of life's challenges head-on and with a sense of purpose. These experiences have involved physically and mentally demanding situations that either I sought out or that confronted me.

In the following chapters, I will share with you several true stories describing such adventures.

These personal accounts demonstrate my determination to overcome assorted challenges outside of the workplace. Based on past as well as recent events, these anecdotes transport you to unusual settings around the world and include some unexpected twists of fate.

Meant to be informative, entertaining, as well as eye-opening, *Taking the Bull by the Horns* will hopefully encourage you to take on whatever life throws at you with aplomb. And in the end, you may agree with me that much is to be gained by sometimes leaving our comfort zones and striding into unfamiliar territory.

CARPE
DIEM

CHAPTER I:
Drop Zone

Talk about starting one's life off with a bang! Madeleine Sophie Barat, a French saint of the Catholic Church, was born in 1779 in the midst of a raging fire that triggered premature labor in her mother. Though born two months premature, Madeleine would go on to found the Society of the Sacred Heart of Jesus, which focuses on the education of girls and women.

Barat College was named after St. Madeleine and started off as an academy for young women in Chicago in 1858. It was moved 35 miles north to Lake Forest in 1904, becoming coeducational in 1982.

When I began my medical school years in the middle to late 1980's, Barat College had some open dormitories to fill and assigned one building for the local medical students. The price and setting were attractive, and many fellow Chicago Medical School students, male and female, joined me in the accommodations at the arts college. It would serve as our home for a good part of our years in medical school.

Early in my second year at Chicago Medical School, I remember a Wednesday evening when some friends had gathered at the Rathskeller. This pub at the school's lower level was frequented by the students as well as faculty and staff members. By then, we students had become accustomed to the long hours of study and what we had signed up for in the road to becoming doctors.

As we downed our cool beers, a dozen of us brainstormed about some group activity that would break the tedium of our classes and life in general. Kendra, a New Yorker who could be the *doppelgänger* of Marisa Tomei, mentioned a ski trip. Butch, a former college wrestler, proposed hang gliding. Our lithe waitress, Carol, said that sailing in Lake Michigan would be part of a perfect day for her.

More ideas were thrown into the mix, some casually and some passionately. After a short period of silence as we ordered more appetizers, I blurted out, "What about skydiving? I've never done it, and I'll bet none of you have either!"

A brief hush permeated the room before some people began expressing interest. One by one, students volunteered that they had either heard of the sport or knew someone who had done it. Word of the conversation spread throughout the busy Rathskeller.

But it was remarkable that not one person present had ventured the actual jumping out of a perfectly good airplane.

Over the next few weeks, rumors about a possible skydiving excursion circulated throughout the medical school. Faculty and staff and students alike discussed the excitement and possible risks and dangers associated with the gest.

Around that time, a study showed that about 30 people died in the United States for every 2 million jumps due to parachuting accidents. In 2007, another report mentioned 18 deaths in 2.2 million jumps, according to the United States Parachute Association. An average of 21 skydiving deaths per year in the United States is another recent statistic.

Keeping these facts in perspective, one should know that the chance of perishing from skydiving is less than the risk of dying while skiing or bicycling. Some even contend that the greatest risk of kicking the bucket on the day of skydiving is on the drive to the airfield!

Two schools of thought emerged regarding the dangers of skydiving. One group felt that the real threat of cutting their medical careers short was not to be ignored. Each of these doctors-to-be felt as uncomfortable as a person wearing shoes two sizes too small. By contrast, the other group remained very interested in pursuing this natural high despite the peril.

Eventually, we medical students residing at Barat told the collegians about our plans for the skydiving escapade. As expected, many expressed a genuine fear as well as curiosity about the extraordinary proposal. After about a week of the news being disseminated around campus, a dozen of the undergraduates were added to our short list.

As time passed, about 20 or so Chicago Medical School students (no faculty) continued to be eager about the big trip, while five Barat collegians stayed firm. The next step was to determine how serious these 25 individuals actually were. Would they walk the walk after having talked the talk?

I began to collect deposits from the interested parties, about $75 each, to allow me to make reservations at a local skydiving facility and to tell me who was really agog about this emprise. I figured that a person willing to part with his/her money was showing a real commitment to me in the big adventure.

When I asked them to make their payments, though, most of the medical students gave me one excuse or another, centering around doubts about the real risks at play. They also became aware that the $75 deposit was not refundable, and that another $50 or more would be needed per person before final arrangements were made.

On the Barat College side, there was a proportionately higher confirmation rate. Of the five eligible students, three were all in, glad to ante up for probably the most thrilling outing thus far in their lives.

For the final count, the "fearless five" were established: Sam and Rex and Thomas from the college, and my colleague Jon and I. A few others were very close to joining us, but they could not quite cough up the money in time. Aware that we had made a bold decision to commit to the skydive, the five of us celebrated by going to a Chicago Blackhawks hockey game that weekend.

Within days, I was calling several airfields in the area, comparing costs and experience with first-time skydivers. Prices were similar in most places, but some organizations dealt with more skydivers and thus boasted more instructors.

After a powwow discussing the various options, we settled on the Sky Knights Sport Parachute Club in East Troy, Wisconsin. This top-notch outfit has initiated many in the world of skydiving since 1963. The drive north to East Troy would take about an hour from Lake Forest, and the excursion would also mark our first foray into the Badger State.

Given our different school schedules, the actual day of the big jump still had to be agreed upon. The weather was becoming colder, and the winter holiday season was only weeks away. Some favored postponing the big day until early the next year.

In a burst of braggadocio, I reminded the others of how trivial they were being. We were about to set forth on arguably the biggest adventure of our lives to date, and they were worried about the winter weather? Jon was with me, and the other three soon came to their senses. After some discussion, all of us set a target date of Saturday, November 22nd.

Preliminary forecasts showed clear skies for that eventful day, with morning temperatures expected in the low to middle 30's Fahrenheit. The Sky Knights contact person told me to remind everyone to wear layered but comfortable clothing and sturdy sneakers for the scheduled jump.

A few short days before the dive, the five of us were obviously excited but also a little apprehensive (that is to say, scared). The updated weather forecast now mentioned possible snow that Saturday. Still, none of us even thought about skipping out – too much pride at stake.

Jon and I decided to do something special to recognize our medical school and colleagues there during the skydiving adventure. Approaching the staff at the Dean's office, we asked what school item we could bring that could admirably represent the Chicago Medical School. After some thought, they suggested a large six-by-four-foot royal purple flag of the institution, with the school seal in the center.

We told the school leaders that we would be honored. The decision was made to take the banner with us for the anticipated jump. Later, though, this seemingly simple plan would turn out to be a little more complicated.

Jump day arrived at last. It was 8 a.m. on November 22nd, and the fearless five awakened to overcast skies but no rain or snow. After a shower and light breakfast, I met the others in front of the medical student dormitory at Barat.

There, we were surprised to see about 30 well-wishers who had come to send us off and say Godspeed and other farewells. A few of the female Barat students shed some tears, but we future skydivers maintained our poise and casual attitude (at least on the outside). Thomas would be driving since he had the most spacious car, a 1976 dark blue Ford Thunderbird that had been his father's. We buckled in as our friends waved to us. Next stop: East Troy.

Approximately halfway to our destination, we had noted no precipitation but the skies were still cloudy. The radio was playing "Highway to Hell" by AC/DC, an all-time energizing classic, but the lyrics were probably not the most appropriate for our emprise that day. Rex later popped in a tape of Lynyrd Skynyrd and skipped to the song "Freebird" to the approval of all. Ten minutes later, my offering was the second Ratt album, and we all first-pumped to the apropos tune "Dangerous but Worth the Risk."

Having crossed into Wisconsin and now about 15 miles from East Troy, we noted the first signs of snowflakes. Looking at each other, all of us wondered if worsening weather was in the offing. The snow remained light, though, and we arrived at the airfield safely. Several ebullient people in jumpsuits with goggles hanging from their necks greeted us.

"Are you with the Aquitania group?"

We nodded and were led to the front office for official business. The waiver forms were no surprise. All of us eventually signed them, being reminded of the small but real danger in the upcoming activity. The next step was deciding the type of skydiving we would be doing that day. The three choices: *static line*, *tandem free fall*, and *accelerated free fall*.

In the least expensive option, static line, the jumper leaves the aircraft at about 3500 feet, and his parachute would open soon after thanks to a static line connected to a secure point on the plane. Said jumper then guides his open parachute to the ground by manipulating the *steering toggles*. The instructional course for static line involved several hours of training. This skydiving option was Sam's initial choice, but he would later change his mind due to peer pressure.

Accelerated free fall (AFF) was the most intense skydiving experience available to us. The training would occupy most of the day, and each trainee by day's end could individually jump off the aircraft at an altitude of 11,000 to 13,000 feet. But he would not be alone.

Once clear of the aircraft, the AFF student is closely accompanied by two certified instructors, also in free fall, who make needed adjustments in the trainee's parachute pack and harness and body position. Once the novice pulls his *rip cord* to open his parachute at about 3500 to 5000 feet, he is expected to steer himself safely to the ground in one piece. Two factors, though, deterred us from this option: money (much more pricey than the other two alternatives) and the time required all day for training.

The advantages of tandem free fall skydiving (TFF), the remaining choice, were unmistakable because of the combination of cost, training time needed, and relative thrill factor. The classroom preparation would only take one or two hours, but we could exit the aircraft as high as 12,000 feet without supplemental oxygen, and the price was only a little more than the static line possibility.

What made all these specifics possible with TFF was that a certified skydiving instructor would be strapped on to the novice, with the front of the tandem master (certified instructor) intimately connected to the back of the beginner.

After we convinced Sam to join the majority, the five of us unanimously gave the thumbs up for TFF. We paid the balance of our bill to the cashier, and two of us also splurged for a videotape to be made of the whole day's experience.

The recording would include the instruction session, how the parachute was packed and then securely fastened to the skydiver, the ride ascending in the aircraft, the actual jump and free fall and parachute opening, and hopefully the final safe landing. Such video evidence of our daring exploits would soon be available for many to see.

As we all began the classroom session, it quickly became clear that a seemingly endless amount of information was being conveyed. Many facts and techniques were covered: the instructor donning the parachute pack and harness, the student putting on his harness, the fitting of helmets and goggles and gloves, maintaining the connection between student and tandem master (THE most important part, in my opinion), ascending on the aircraft, jumping off the plane, practicing correct technique during free fall, pulling of the rip cord, and skillfully descending to the ground with the parachute open.

Even though he was strapped on to the instructor throughout the entire skydive, the student had the opportunity to control his descent to some degree. If the amateur skydiver was capable and self-confident, he would be allowed to do as much of the free fall steering and pulling of the rip cord and landing activities as he was comfortable with.

The class in the Sky Knights Sport Parachute Club central building seemed endless, but we all stayed attentive and fascinated. Many safety points were punctuated during the talk. And the expert teacher, Brad, patiently answered our myriad of questions.

Almost an hour and a half into his presentation, Brad asked if there was anything else he could clarify or needed to explain. Once silence filled the room, we knew the session was over.

"Upward and onward!" exclaimed Jon, after which we all raised our fists toward the ceiling.

At that moment, we all felt certain that this adventure which originated in the Rathskeller a few months prior was really going to happen.

The five of us were then directed to an area where our gear was put in place. Afterwards, we followed the five tandem masters, pilot, and videographers to the small aircraft on the tarmac. I carried the large Chicago Medical School flag, planning to open the banner after I jumped off the plane so the videotape would show it during free fall and the descent to terra firma.

That was the idea.

We all hopped in, each claiming a space on the floor of the aircraft. The engines roared, and the small plane began to move slowly as we awaited clearance from the control tower.

"You're cleared for takeoff," said the air traffic controller, and our pilot revved the engines. The next thing we knew we were airborne.

As the two-engine plane climbed slowly to the heavens, uneasy banter among us newbies filled the air. Meanwhile, the five tandem masters got busy and began to arrange the connections between each beginner and his respective certified instructor.

Before long, I noted that my altimeter showed 10,000 feet. Jake, the head/senior skydiver on board, then asked who wanted to jump first.

Ever since plans for this gest were put in motion, the relatively minor detail of who would be the first person to jump was the one thing the five of us had not discussed. Certainly, the first one off the plane would command much respect because of an apparent fearlessness of the relative unknown. On the downside, the initial jumper would also have the first chance to get cold feet under the pressure.

With my adrenaline level running high, knowing that I was the one spearheading this whole risky endeavor, and sensing a general hesitation in the air, I instinctively announced, "See you on the ground, boys!" to the relief of the others.

I inched toward the opening on the starboard side of the plane, connected to my very important tandem master, who happened to be Jake. My fellow thrill-seekers patted me on the back but remained silent.

The medical school flag was held close to me, as if I cradled a child. Next, I heard Jake say, "It's that time."

Approaching the point from which I would dive off the aircraft, I saw some light snow falling and felt a chill up my spine.

Several thoughts now surfaced. Is this going to be more dangerous than I expected? Will the snow fall on the parachutes and make them ineffective? Why was I thinking about voluntarily jumping out of a perfectly functional airplane in the first place?

Aware of my indecision, Jake took the opportunity to tell me that he had gone on skydiving trips many a time under these circumstances. My tandem master expressed his words with candidness and self-assuredness. Soon after, I decided to throw caution to the wind (pun intended).

I shilly-shallied for only a New York minute before jumping off the airplane with my instructor fastened to my back. An instant later, I felt like a boulder dropping at light speed toward Earth. The videographer exited the small aircraft seconds after Jake and me, continuing to take footage of my busy day.

Once I realized that I was falling toward the big blue marble, I reached for the flag (held by my right arm) with my other hand. My attempt to open the school banner was futile, however, because of the strong forces of air moving the fabric in various directions. If I had not tied a corner of the flag to my right wrist during the plane's ascent, it would have been lost in the Earth's atmosphere by now.

The banner was interfering with Jake's vision, so I held it in the form of a small ball for the time being. We were descending at over 120 to 130 miles per hour during free fall, and I was experiencing a combination of exhilaration and fear and satisfaction all at once.

Recalling what I had learned in the classroom, I spread my left arm out wide, as if it was a wing. My other hand was held near my torso, holding the flag. As I moved at breakneck speed through the cold air thanks to the planet's gravitational pull, terminal velocity was soon reached. I was no longer accelerating but my body was still hurtling at a constant speed of over 100 miles per hour toward the drop zone.

In this state of free fall, I felt like I was flying (or maybe floating) with the slight upward pressure of air on my body and face. And all I could hear were the strong loud winds around me.

After an unbelievable minute of traveling faster than a fastball thrown by Aroldis Chapman, I felt a tap on my shoulder. As I had been instructed, I glanced at the blurry readout on my altimeter, and it showed 4000 feet. Reaching for the rip cord, I finally deployed the parachute at 3500 feet. A force of sudden deceleration was felt as I knew the parachute had opened successfully. At that juncture, I was able to open the school flag and give the videographer a good view of me holding up the Chicago Medical School colors.

The frantic pace of free fall was replaced with a relatively peaceful sense of well-being as we floated slowly toward firm ground. Buildings appeared ever larger as the descent continued, and light snow was still falling around me.

Again, I squeezed the flag into the form of a ball held close to my body as I grabbed the steering toggles to prepare for landing. Once accustomed to the controls, I was able to turn in any direction as Jake corrected my technique.

We touched down almost right at the large red-and-white target marked on the ground, but the landing was mildly rough. Underestimating the speed at which we were traveling, I slid forward on impact, landing on my bum instead of my feet, taking Jake down with me.

I tried to stand up. It felt odd to be on my feet on the hard ground after I had experienced virtual weightlessness during most of my dive toward the Sky Knights target zone. My sense of equilibrium was momentarily lost as I struggled to stay upright on the cold earth. Seconds later, the ability to balance myself returned.

The videographer and Jake shook my hand, and I perceived a sense of euphoria despite the mild ache in my lower back. The connections between Jake's parachute pack and harness and my harness were removed and the intact parachute was carefully detached from Jake's gear.

Jon and his tandem master were now approaching the drop zone, and my brown-haired colleague from Arizona let out a loud "Yeah! Yeah!" They had a near-perfect landing, staying on their feet.

After they made contact with the ground, and even before they were disconnected from each other, I managed to run over and give each of them a high five. The two of us first-time skydivers agreed that what had just transpired was more thrilling than expected and well worth the small risk we had accepted.

Meanwhile, snow was falling on our faces and covered the ground around us. We looked upward at the rest of our group.

Despite the steady precipitation, Rex then Sam then Thomas safely made it to the drop zone and were met with congratulatory cheers from several fellow skydivers. Some landings were not pretty, but no injuries were sustained.

All five of us were lightly blanketed in snow once we reached the main building of the Sky Knights Sport Parachute Club. Certificates were handed out to everyone, and videotapes were being processed for Jon and me.

The fearless five later mafficked with the traditional pizza and beer at a local tavern. We had come to experience what relatively few dared to do, and our uneasiness was now replaced with exaltation. Looking over the jukebox selections, I put in two quarters for the tune "Fly Like an Eagle" by the Steve Miller Band.

In the midst of our celebration, our comely waitress joined us in a group picture. She also surprised us with the fact that she had also been a student at the Sky Knights Club, with her first skydive taking place about three months prior with two of her friends. We exchanged numbers and discussed a potential future skydive date.

Over the next few months, those videotapes of Jon and me would be viewed by dozens of friends and acquaintances. Pictures of the big day (also taken by the videographer) were also shown around the medical school and college campuses.

The Chicago Medical School administration officials were grateful when we presented them with a framed picture of the school flag held by yours truly as I was gliding to the ground attached to a parachute. Students heard about our stories and admired our boldness, but most were still not ready to take the dive. I realized that this sport is clearly not everyone's cup of tea.

In the ten years or so after my East Troy escapade, I went skydiving about a dozen more times, sometimes with the tandem option and other times doing the more rigorous accelerated free fall program. Each outing involved different groups of friends and thrill-seekers, and only one injury (a fractured foot) has occurred during those excursions (with no fatalities).

As I became more proficient, advanced maneuvers during free fall, including turns and twists and flips, were possible. In addition, my know-how has allowed me to relay some pointers to more junior skydivers.

You may ask who actually goes skydiving, other than daring medical students and college students. People of all ages and occupations have been among the participants. And one does not have to be as ambitious as the Austrian daredevil Felix Baumgartner, who jumped 128,000 feet (!) on October 14th 2012. But this extreme sport does require reasonably good health, planning, mental focus, safety awareness, and a sense of adventure.

More importantly, what makes someone want to jump off a perfectly functioning airplane and barrel toward Earth at incredible velocities? Unforgettable thrills and memories like nothing else.

Over Taft, California

CHAPTER II:
26.2

According to fable, Pheidippides, a Greek soldier, ran nonstop from the ancient city of Marathon to Athens in 490 B.C. to report on the Greeks' victory over the much larger Persian army at the Battle of Marathon. The distance from Marathon to Athens spanned 26.2 miles, and Pheidippides was said to have collapsed once arriving at Athens. Though this skirmish was a defining moment in the Greco-Persian Wars, showing that the immense Persian military force could be defeated, it is now better known as the origin of the modern day marathon footrace.

In the past, a long-distance race like the marathon was not on my bucket list. As a matter of fact, I used to eschew running for the sake of running. During my high school years, running served as a tool or necessity for other sports, such as basketball or tennis. Endurance in jogging or running was not my forte, but I was a fair sprinter on the track. For these reasons, I focused on sports having much start-and-stop activity.

When a man does something out of his nature, though, a frequent reason is a woman in his life. As an example of this point, I ran my first marathon several years ago thanks to my girlfriend Sienna. At the time, I, a nonrunner if ever one existed, was dared by said lady to complete the local San Diego Marathon that was a few months away. She was positive I would find a way to sidestep the challenge, but I considered her proposition – to a large part because she agreed to do a dare of mine if I succeeded. After some degree of cajoling by her, I accepted the invitation.

Big things often have small beginnings. Based on this hypothesis, in order to get a grasp of the magnitude of running 26.2 miles, I first set out to walk this distance. I measured out a route that spanned about six miles and speed walked the designated path four times in succession. This endeavor took me several hours and was surprisingly manageable, except for blisters appearing on the bottoms of my feet. It was my assumption that the long distance covered caused the painful condition.

After waiting a week or so for the blisters to heal, it was my goal to get started on running at a relatively slow pace to assess my endurance. Not accustomed to this aerobic activity, though, I found that even slow running for a long distance made me breathless.

It soon became clear that the best tactic was to run until I felt winded, take a brief walking break, then repeat the cycle for the length of the distance planned. Eventually, I ran and walked a total of 15 miles on a given day. Other than some mild soreness in the leg muscles, the main problem was again the foot blisters.

In an effort to solve the blister condition, I decided to call my younger brother Ron, a veteran of 50 marathons. Through it all, he has remarkably sustained no major injuries and never entered the medical tent at any marathon event.

He was amused at my question and asked me what type of shoes I was running with, knowing I was an avid basketball player. Nike Air sneakers was my answer.

Ron opined that it would be prudent for me to purchase some well-fitted running shoes, which are lighter and provide better ventilation than court shoes. In addition, special running socks were a good accessory to lessen the friction between foot and shoe. He predicted that my blister problem would be solved in no time.

Off I went to Road Runner Sports, a local store specializing in running shoes and related sportswear and gear. During a personal evaluation by one of the staff, I was told about my arch and stride as I ran on the treadmill. Several shoes were suggested to go well with my style of running.

I ended up purchasing the Asics TN745 running shoe with a customized insole. To lessen blister risk even more, special layered socks and Body Glide (an anti-blister and anti-chafing roll-on applied to the soles and other sensitive areas) were also acquired. It is with pride to say that I have experienced no foot blisters ever since.

Now able to run without the threat of nagging blisters, I slowly increased the amount of running relative to walking during my training sessions. In a few weeks, it was possible for me to run almost five miles before a walking break was needed.

By then, the local marathon was about a month away, so I started to train more frequently, about three times a week. Not wanting to carry a water bottle if possible, I ran routes that had water fountains along the way. For carbohydrate fuel during a strenuous training session, small packets of semi-liquid energy gels were kept in my shorts pockets.

Weeks passed, and as the marathon date approached, Sienna was impressed by my progress but also concerned – she would be obligated to fulfill her end of the bargain (a dare suggested by me) if I successfully finished the race in the time allotted.

I reassured her that my challenge or dare for her, assuming I completed the marathon race, would be fair and possibly enjoyable. Sienna was somewhat relieved by my words but still wondered if something sneaky was on my mind.

On the week before race day, it was evident that I could run about seven or eight miles without a walking break. No blisters were in sight, and leg soreness was relatively mild. Taking my brother Ron's advice, I did no running in the week before the marathon, save a five-mile jog.

Expo Day for the San Diego Marathon arrived, and I was accompanied by Ron, who opted to fly down from San Francisco to also participate in the race. At the fair, I would get my bib number, timing chip, and pre-race goodie bag. In the bag were my official marathon T-shirt, small nutritional packets, and advertisements for upcoming races and miscellaneous running products.

Also at the sports fair, experienced marathoners conducted small informational sessions for novice runners, with advice on maintaining hydration and carbohydrate nutrition. No one wanted any of the first-time runners to become depleted of sugar and water to the point of *hitting the wall*.

In the marathon or any other endurance event, the low-carbohydrate phenomenon of *hitting the wall* can include symptoms such as generalized body heaviness, numbness, poor coordination, and slow thinking. One way to avoid this powerless condition is to maintain a smart balance among conditioning, pace of running, carbohydrate intake, and water intake.

At the expo, most people attending were in a happy mood, visiting various vendors promoting sportswear and nutritional products and gadgets to help the endurance athlete. There were a significant number, though, who appeared serious and businesslike.

"These guys and gals are probably high-strung elite marathoners," I told Ron.

I bought a commemorative marathon cap and a refrigerator magnet at the main shop before we went to dinner. It was advisable to have a generous amount of carbohydrates at this last big meal before the race, my brother told me.

At the restaurant, my brother and I took in some hearty helpings of pasta and meatballs. He told me stories of some of his past marathons, each of which he remembered vividly.

For instance, during one of his races at Napa, California, Ron stopped to help a fellow runner on the ground. He recalls she was wearing a fuchsia top and black shorts.

Britney was a 5-foot-5 brunette paralegal who developed a leg cramp at mile 19 of the race. One minute she was running to the sounds of the song "Kashmir" by Led Zeppelin on her iPod. In the next instant, this marathoner was on the pavement because of extreme right calf pain.

Ron temporarily halted his run and offered to help Britney, who responded, "Anything to stop the pain!"

He asked her to remove her shoe and began to massage her very tight calf. Eventually, the cramp went away after several minutes. She was able to resume the race soon after, grateful to my brother. After Ron and then Britney successfully completed the race, they dated for about six months.

Once I finished my carbohydrate-rich supper, my girlfriend called and wished both me and my brother good luck. She would not be able to make it to the marathon event because of a family emergency.

Ron told me to try to get some good sleep that night but warned that such a task was no small feat. Soon enough, I discovered his wisdom. The marathon would start around 7 a.m. for us, so we hit the hay about 9 p.m. However, for the life of me, it was almost impossible to fall asleep.

I drank some warm milk, watched a relaxing TV show for several minutes, moved to a bed in another room, did some light reading – everything short of going to the pharmacy and buying a sleeping pill. Still, no slumber.

Evidently, two main factors were at play here: unusually early sleep time and unusually high adrenaline levels.

With the marathon beginning at 7 a.m. the next day, I figured it would be sensible to leave my house by 5:30 a.m. to allow for transportation time, parking, and unexpected delays. Such an early start meant that I should retire at 9 p.m. the night before to get a good night's sleep. But my body wasn't ready to call it a day, since it was rare on a Saturday night for me to fall asleep before midnight. My internal clock was telling me that it would not let my body shut down for the night just yet.

The anticipation of my first marathon also revved up my brain as I lay in bed. As a result of this nighttime adrenaline rush, I fell victim to a faster heart rate and higher level of alertness than usual. In this state of mind, attaining sleep was not going to be easy.

My radio's digital clock now showed 11 p.m., which quickly became midnight, then 1 a.m. (you get the idea). By then, I was fearful that only three more hours remained before my alarm would chime at 4:30 a.m. More racing thoughts appeared, further denying me the important rest I needed before a grueling first marathon.

Come 2 a.m., I realized that getting any quality sleep that night had become a pipe dream. I settled for lying down and closing my eyes to at least give my peepers a rest.

The loud voice of a radio show host startled me as my alarm clock sounded at around 4:30 a.m. I struggled to arise from bed to prepare for the big day. A lukewarm shower, though, gave me back my vigor.

I had a bagel with peanut butter washed down with some milk. Before long, Ron and I were leaving my home and off to the race. A few miles down the freeway, we encountered traffic. I thought to myself: Who is awake at 5:30 in the morning on a Sunday?

It dawned on me that these cars were being driven by my fellow marathoners and probably spectators and race personnel and volunteers. Later, I would find out that almost 16,000 runners finished the marathon that year.

After waiting almost fifteen minutes in the logjam, I noticed that a few cars were taking an early exit off the freeway. Deciding to follow these moving vehicles, I soon gladly discovered that they were leading Ron and me by way of side streets to the race parking lot, bypassing the highway congestion. We quickly found a parking spot, then my brother and I hopped on a shuttle bus headed for the starting line.

Ron and I reached the starting area about 30 minutes before the race and were witness to thousands of runners and race staff being cheered on by the crowd. It was a celebration for everyone except the thousands of participants about to begin a long ordeal that day.

We attached our bib numbers to our shirts and the timing chips to our shoes. These chips would mark our arrivals at various points along the race course, recording our progress throughout the event. Our relatively early arrival at the start line also gave us enough time to wait in the long queues for the portable toilets before the race.

At long last, the gun sounded and I joined a myriad of runners aiming to cover 26.2 miles. The excitement of my first marathon and the wildly vocal crowd gave me an enormous energy lift. At first, I seemed to be running effortlessly among the many participants.

I kept pace with Ron for a mile or two before he moved ahead, showing his experience and endurance. My early fast pace was possible because of encouragement by the crowd, but the rest of the race would be up to me.

It felt like an hour had passed before I reached the first water station (it was in reality only 20 minutes), and the stop for water was an excuse for me to take a brief walking break. Refreshed after ingesting much-needed fluids, I resumed running at a comfortable pace.

As I progressed through my first marathon, the distance between runners became longer and longer. My first side cramp occurred ten miles into the contest, just below my ribs on the right. Many explanations have been proposed for this discomfort, including decreased blood flow to the liver or diaphragm with strenuous exercise. After walking for a minute, the pain subsided.

To avoid another cramp, I concentrated on my breathing technique, trying to get in as much oxygen as possible. My preference was breathing in for three steps, then exhaling for three steps, and repeating the pattern. Another side stitch or cramp appeared about 18 miles into the footrace, and walking for a minute or two worked again.

With each mile run during the competition, large signs telling the athletes the number of miles completed were in full view along the course. I knew I was making steady progress one mile at a time. By the 23rd mile, though, it became clear that I had *hit the wall*.

In this condition, I was mildly lightheaded and my body seemed to weigh 500 pounds as I struggled to run forward. I had been ingesting my carbohydrate gels about every two to three miles and making brief stops at the water stations at those times, but could I have underestimated my body's energy needs?

As I mentioned earlier, the uncomfortable event known as *hitting the wall* occurs when the body's reserves of glycogen in the liver and muscles become virtually depleted during an endurance race. The effects of this hypoglycemia may include loss of energy and extreme lightheadedness and even hallucinations at times. And experienced as well as novice endurance athletes can fall victim to this distress.

My buddy Gary, who has conquered a marathon and several triathlons (including the Half Ironman distance), has hit the wall on at least a few occasions. He relates one occurring during a training run on a hot Florida day. The image of a German shepherd moving in his path was very vivid, but this vision just as quickly "disappeared into thin air" as he recollects. In another incident, he glimpsed the fleeting picture of a kangaroo-sized rabbit with extra-large ears on the side of the road. It is important to know that he is quite the animal lover.

Gary fell victim to yet another such occurrence about three-quarters into the final running stage of the Rhoto's Half Ironman Triathlon in Oceanside, California. He admits to having expended a lot of energy on the bicycle (second) phase of the race, leading to extreme fatigue and hallucinations toward the end of the contest. These altered perceptions included him feeling like he was traveling through a wormhole, much like Jodie Foster's character Ellie Arroway in the 1997 science fiction movie *Contact*.

Becoming aware of my carbohydrate-depleted state, I had no choice but to walk and wait for the next water station. There were carbohydrate gel packets in my pocket, but water had to be ingested with each packet to promote its optimal digestion and absorption.

About three minutes later, still moving at a slow walking pace, I spotted the familiar sight of runners slowing down. Undoubtedly, a water booth was nearby. Taking in the contents of a gel pack, I washed the semi-liquid down with two cups of water. Within seconds, a wave of energy permeated my entire body and my mind became sharper. Three miles to go.

The last few miles of a marathon are clearly the most punishing. By then, one's muscles and maybe joints are sore, blisters may have formed on the feet (not mine, though), and there is the awareness that 30 or more minutes of running still remain before the finish.

Well-wishing spectators along the course make that final stretch a little easier. "You are doing great!" and "Only a few more miles until home!" and "You can do this!" were among the encouraging comments I heard during this state of fatigue. They helped me fight off the temptation to just walk to the finish line.

Before long, I took a gander at the sign that indicated "25 MILES," meaning only 1.2 miles separated me from the finish line. Since I was already exhausted and sore, it would have been easy for me to slow down and jog for the rest of the race. But I managed to convince myself that barely completing the marathon and slowly crossing the finish line would not do.

A sprint in the last 400 yards or so was in order. If I could pull this dash off, I could easily pass dozens of runners who were likely too spent at that last stage of the race. If I could finish at a good pace, I would also have the personal satisfaction of knowing my stamina was good to the end.

After taking in my last carbohydrate gel pack at the final water station, I accelerated as much as was possible and began to pass one tired athlete after another. Knowing that the finish line was in sight, I put up with the muscle soreness and hard breathing in my drive past other marathoners.

My stride lengthened in the last 100 yards despite the pain. In the end, I just got past a fading runner as my timing chip triggered the final sensor.

It is difficult to know exactly what drove me to turn it on at the end, risking more pain and possibly a late stumble and fall.

A surge of adrenaline knowing the ordeal was almost over? The desire to show spectators and other participants my late-race endurance and strength? Pride in passing runners to improve my finish time and overall place among the many athletes? Wanting to look good in my photo at the finish line?

I suspect all of the above motivated me to varying degrees.

In the area past the finish line, my brother Ron, who had completed his race quite a while before me, gave me a strong congratulatory handshake and a bottle of water. My muscles felt like they were burning and my face and arms were likely sunburned. Due to tightness and soreness in my legs, I walked like a man who had just undergone a vasectomy. Still, the satisfaction of attaining my goal trumped all these hardships.

Slowly moving around the festive post-race area, I commended fellow marathoners, all draped with finishers' medals around their necks, and all with wide smiles. We proudly walked around as if we had just won Olympic medals, ready to go on the dais to wave to the fans.

This achievement was the first for many that day, and we newbies knew we had just persevered in an insane run that covered the length of over 460 football fields. I later found out that no one died during the footrace, but dozens suffered from overuse injuries and dehydration.

Why did we all do it? Well, I can tell you it was not just for the medals.

Don't ever underestimate the appeal of achievement. After San Diego, I set out to do another marathon, to prove I was not a one-and-done kind of guy. And after that race, the challenge of running another event and the encouragement from friends made along the way urged me to do yet another.

All told, I would finish eight marathons in that first year, with the eighth one only two weeks after the seventh. Following that year, five more marathon races were in the books before I closed that chapter in my sports career.

After my inaugural one in San Diego, the Pasadena Marathon would have to be among the most memorable. For the first half of the race, rain poured down, sometimes heavily. But everyone continued on. Some wore large clear or green garbage bags as makeshift rain gear. Others were prepared with waterproof running attire. The rest, like me, got soaked from head to foot.

That was not the fastest marathon for any of us.

Las Vegas was another 26.2 miles to remember. With the desert climate and the race starting at five or six in the morning in early December, temperatures were in the 30's Fahrenheit for the first hour or two of the event. As a result, I had to wear gloves until the 6th mile of the contest. Still, despite those frigid conditions, several runners had the audacity to wear only shorts and tank tops for the competition!

There would be no heat strokes that day.

If the word can be used to describe a marathon race, my most "pleasant" marathon experiences took place in the area of Palos Verdes, a group of coastal cities about 30 minutes south of downtown Los Angeles.

The Boston Marathon is the nation's oldest annual marathon, going back to 1897. But the Palos Verdes Marathon was the second-oldest continuously run marathon in the country, taking place for about 45 years.

I have performed best in this relatively small marathon for several reasons. The Palos Verdes Marathon was primarily a local affair, with somewhere between 200 and 300 participants a year when I was competing. Nonetheless, it was the scene for serious runners hoping to qualify for the Boston event. And since it involved less than 300 athletes on average, registration was held only a few hours before race time on a Sunday morning (with no required expo the day before), making it very convenient.

Other factors that made this competition attractive involved the race course itself. The path was set in the gentle rolling hills of Palos Verdes, with a soothing sea breeze and cool temperatures (the event was usually held in May). Views of the Pacific Ocean and cliffs and handsome mansions lined the route. Finally, that time of year turned out to be best for my training schedule.

Alas, due to economic reasons, only a half marathon was run in 2012, and plans for 2013 were not yet finalized at the time of this book's printing.

My last marathon was completed in 2010 (for reasons that will become apparent later in this book), but I remain friends with marathoners and other runners that I have met along the way. They still tell me about their challenging races, and my brother Ron continues to encourage me to hit the road for another 26.2 miles. I do not envy the continued wear and tear on their legs, though.

An interesting piece of trivia: That Asics TN745 running shoe purchased before my first marathon has been through all 13 of my marathons *and* training runs! Experts tell me that a well-maintained running shoe has a lifetime of up to 500 miles. My marathon races alone add up to almost 350 miles. In my estimation, the longevity of my Asics TN745 is a testament to both my careful avoidance of overtraining for these demanding races as well as the durability of Asics products.

Looking back at my marathon years, many fond memories have etched themselves in my brain. The anticipation of race days, early morning awakenings on said days, the sight of hundreds or thousands of other runners doing the same, and the buzz and blare of the crowds on a Sunday morning. Fleeting conversations with fellow marathoners during the races, dating someone I met after the finish of one event, and cheerful volunteers at the water stations who sometimes also passed out orange slices. And of course, there is "the runner's high."

Something I always found curious about marathons: In those last 300 yards, as you sense the imminent accomplishment, the pains in your legs due to two dozen miles of running mysteriously disappear! And seconds later, once you cross the finish line after 26 miles and 385 yards of blood, sweat, and tears, you truly feel like you are on top of the world.

The San Francisco Marathon

CHAPTER III:
Night Flight

Scenic Budapest on the Danube River is a charming destination and a modern city of contrasts. The geographically flat and lively half of this metropolis, Pest, lies across the water from the more leafy and traditional half, Buda, which stands on a vast hill. Pest is home to St. Stephen's Basilica, Parliament, and much of the city's commerce. Buda boasts the historic and magnificent Buda Castle (also known as the Royal Palace and Royal Castle) and the Fisherman's Bastion, from which one can take in panoramic views of the city.

In St. Stephen's Basilica lies the unique attraction of the gruesome mummified fist of Hungary's first king, Stephen I. Grand lion statues guard the two ends of the historic Chain Bridge that traverses the Danube to connect Buda and Pest. And from Gellért Hill, where a massive statue of Bishop Gellért faces the Danube, one beholds an awesome vista of the city and famous river.

After a busy but enjoyable one-week vacation in this attractive capital city, my girlfriend Sienna and I felt refreshed and enlightened. We knew, however, that a long journey home would follow, consisting of a lengthy transatlantic ride to Chicago O'Hare International Airport and then a shorter domestic trip to San Diego, California.

We arrived about two hours before our scheduled flight at the Budapest Ferenc Liszt International Airport, a modern facility that offers Wi-Fi technology, a post office, and a chapel. Before the long trip to Chicago, Sienna and I sat down at an airport restaurant and enjoyed a tasty final helping of Hungarian cuisine: *csirkepaprikás* (spicy chicken) with some domestic beer. Our flight was on time, and we were soon airborne without incident.

Our travel across Europe and then the Atlantic went relatively smoothly. A couple of films, two reasonably flavorsome meals, and some games on the personal airline monitors were pleasant enough. On board, Sienna and I casually reviewed some of the digital photos taken by us all over Budapest.

Once we reached Chicago O'Hare at around 7 p.m., electronic displays showed our connecting flight to San Diego to be about two hours away. We knew, though, that this airport was notorious for flight delays, not unusual since it is the fourth busiest airport in the world.

Strolling around the terminal, my girlfriend and I admired some of the artwork at the airport, which is named after "Butch" O'Hare, the United States Navy's first fighter ace in World War II. He received the Medal of Honor from President Franklin Roosevelt for shooting down five Japanese bombers in 1942. We purchased some souvenirs at a gift shop, and we eventually arrived at the gate area for our flight home.

To our surprise, an announcement that our flight was on time sounded overhead. Weary due to the day of travel and the evening hour, Sienna and I ambled to the gate and then into the airliner before finding our assigned seats. We turned off our cell phones and awaited the flight attendant's safety demonstration.

Once her speech was over, cabin lights were dimmed and the 767 aircraft was ready for takeoff. The engines grumbled as the plane gained speed on the runway before we were officially in the air. Sienna fell asleep seconds later. I drifted into a dreamless nothingness in my comfortable seat.

The pleasant but firm voice of a stewardess abruptly tore me out of a seemingly brief slumber (in actuality, we had already been flying 30,000 feet above ground level for over two hours). Her tone on the public address system relayed a sense of urgency.

The message was a summons to any willing passenger who was qualified to treat a medical emergency. Battling my desire to return to sleep, I nonetheless opted to lay my finger on the lighted overhead button. Within seconds, flight attendant Amy appeared. To me, she bore a resemblance to a blonde Sela Ward.

"Good evening, sir. Can I help you?"

I told Amy that I was a physician and asked her to give me the skinny on the medical situation. She first requested identification, after which I pulled out the wallet copy of my medical license and my passport. Meanwhile, Sienna continued her apparently deep sleep, not awakened by the sounds around her.

Grinning as she perused my papers, Amy asked me to follow her. Overhead lights were now illuminated in the cabin as I heard mumbling among the passengers. In addition, personal overhead lights were turned on in an area a few rows down.

The cabin crew member stopped at the brightly lit row and introduced me to the couple of Greta and Max, both in their 60's. Greta was clearly in some mild respiratory distress while Max was anxiously able to shake my hand. He said hello with a thick German accent.

I asked if he spoke much English, to which he responded hesitantly, "Just a little."

None of the flight or cabin crew spoke German, Amy revealed. So I asked her to make an announcement to find a passenger who spoke fluent German and English. Not a soul responded. I then thought to myself that this situation would be more challenging than expected.

I had taken some German classes in high school and college, excited to use this practical knowledge in my past trips to Germany, Austria, and Switzerland. However, those excursions had occurred a few years back and my ability to apply this language skill would understandably be very rusty now.

"*Guten abend, wie geht es Ihnen*? *Ich bin ein Arzt, und ich versuchen zu helfen,*" I stated, asking how the couple was and introducing myself as a doctor trying to help.

Thinking I was fluent in his native tongue, Max responded in rapid German, too fast for me to understand.

I asked him to speak slowly, after which he said, "My wife…dizzy…some trouble with breathe. No help with candy I give her."

"*Welche Medikamente zu nehmen Ihrer Frau*?" (What medicines does your wife take?) I asked.

The man looked into his wife's bag but found no pills or medication list. He then told me she might have her pills in the overhead luggage.

"*Hat sie Schmerzen in Kopf oder Brust*? *Rauchen sie Zigaretten*?" (Does she have a headache or chest pain, and does she smoke cigarettes?)

He shook his head.

I asked Amy for a stethoscope, and she produced one within a minute. Meanwhile, another flight attendant had joined us. Jean was in her late 20's and had strawberry blonde hair.

Greta was still not speaking much, and her pulse was found to be fast at 120 and mildly faint. Her forehead did not feel warm. Placing the stethoscope on her chest, I was unable to hear any breath sounds, probably because the airplane cabin noise made it impossible.

Next, Jean brought me a blood pressure machine at my request. Still, with the ambient noise, I could not discern any reading with the stethoscope on her upper arm as I tried to use the sphygmomanometer. Fortunately, I was able to measure her systolic blood pressure by using the blood pressure cuff and taking her radial pulse. It read 100 (millimeters of mercury), not bad but not far from being low.

Further cursory examination of Greta showed equal-sized pupils, good eye movements, no facial droop, and no fever. Her face was mildly pale, but the blood pressure measurement told me she was getting enough blood flow to her brain, at least for now. However, her lightheadedness, mild trouble breathing, and elevated pulse were concerns.

Immediately, we were able to start the patient on some supplemental oxygen that was available on board. Unfortunately, her dizziness only improved by a small amount with this treatment. Also, she began to complain of mild nausea as she spoke to her husband in a very soft voice.

The cabin crew and I decided to move our patient to the relatively quiet galley area, giving me a better chance of listening to her lungs with the stethoscope. Greta was barely able to bear weight on her legs, though, and her stout frame required three of us to transport her. In the process, we were creating quite a stir among the now awake passengers.

The noise was clearly less as she lay flat on the galley floor, but it was still too loud for me to hear Greta's lung sounds. I asked Amy if an even quieter place was available in the airplane. She hesitated for a moment, then Jean exclaimed, "What about next to the cockpit area?"

Amy nodded and Greta was on the move once again. By now, her pulse had risen to 130 and her face was a little more pale. Fortunately, her systolic blood pressure was stable. A blanket was used to cover our patient as she was now shivering. I checked her overall strength, and it was equal in all limbs. I also noted no swelling or tenderness in her legs.

Once we arrived near the cockpit, we laid Greta down. At that point, Amy executed a series of knocks on the door. I was told that since the September 11th attacks on the World Trade Center and Pentagon, cockpit doors on all American commercial flights have been locked from the inside while the plane is in the air.

After a few seconds, the copilot emerged. He spoke with Amy briefly before the door was locked once again. They were discussing the severity of Greta's condition and if she needed to get to a hospital as soon as possible.

At last, I was able to hear some breath sounds with the stethoscope. They were normal and now easily heard, and there were no indications of fluid in the lungs. However, her heart rate had risen to 140 now.

Greta then whispered to Max, who said to me, "*Sehr schwindlig*." He was telling me she was becoming very lightheaded.

At that point, a repeat blood pressure measurement, this time possible with the machine since the ambient noise level was low, showed numbers of 90/50, a clearly low reading. With all the information available to me, I concluded she was probably dehydrated, so I elevated her legs while keeping her body flat on the ground. Less likely possibilities included pulmonary embolism (blood clot in lung) and myocardial infarction (heart attack).

Again, the copilot unlocked the cockpit door and talked with Amy. The copilot asked me if he should land the airplane prematurely to get the ill passenger to a hospital sooner than later. Looking at Greta with her worsening blood pressure, elevated pulse, lightheadedness, and mild breathing difficulty, I was strongly considering that option. Could she have a fulminant illness?

If you are the type of person who likes the spotlight, you would have loved to be in my shoes at that instant. A crucial decision had to be made, with a life in the balance. In addition, there was the question of whether Greta's condition was serious enough to justify an early landing for the airliner to get her to a hospital. Such a diversion would impact the travel plans of all the passengers on board.

Meanwhile, Max had managed to get the pill bottles of Greta's medicines from her luggage in the overhead bin. Looking over the bottles, I realized she was taking some pills for gout and acid reflux, along with blood pressure medicines that included a diuretic.

Handling this difficult situation with aplomb was a challenge, but I maintained my mental focus thanks to the excitement of the moment. I decided to ask Jean what other medical supplies were available in the aircraft. She quickly left and returned with the in-flight medical kit.

A plan came to mind after I surveyed the medical treatments and supplies laid out in front of me. I told the cabin crew and copilot that my answer to the question of whether the 767 should land earlier than previously scheduled will come in a few minutes.

Jean was instructed to prepare some of the materials in the kit. She opened the container of the IV saline bag as directed and connected the tubing. Elevating the bag, she was asked to be ready.

Using the alcohol swabs and gloves and tourniquet, I prepared Greta's arm and warned her before thrusting the IV catheter needle into the best vein I could find. The appearance of dark blood in the catheter's plastic applicator chamber told me that I had successfully entered a vein. Slowly, I advanced the apparatus further into the vein, simultaneously withdrawing the needle.

Once the catheter was pushed to its limit, I put pressure on the overlying skin and carefully removed the needle and then the catheter applicator. Next, the tourniquet was taken off, and the IV tubing (held by Jean) was connected to the catheter. I released the pressure on the vein and taped down the catheter-IV tubing combination. Jean adjusted the IV valve to the wide-open position and saline flowed freely into Greta's vein.

Now it was time to wait. Silence pierced the air as everyone's eyes were on our German patient. I was checking her pulse, which initially did not change.

Soon, though, signs of clear improvement became apparent. Within a couple of minutes, Greta was beginning to talk more and her face pinked up.

She mumbled, "*Gefühl besser*" (She was feeling better).

More words were expressed by Greta, but I could not comprehend any of them. Max moved close to her and they spoke in German. He reported that she was asking why she was on the floor and what were all these people doing around her. Everyone smiled and gave a mild cheer.

Repeat measurements showed that her pulse had improved to 90 beats per minute and her blood pressure had risen to a normal 120/70. She was breathing comfortably by now and no longer dizzy. For the first time tonight, Greta asked for something to drink.

I congratulated the entire cabin crew and praised them for a job well done. Everyone had remained calm and collected during this entire in-flight emergency. But despite our patient's improvement, I asked everyone to remain alert, since she was still not completely out of the woods.

The pilot trumpeted overhead that the aircraft would be landing in San Diego within an hour as planned and that no unscheduled detour would be needed. The announcement was greeted with applause from those passengers still awake. Word eventually spread that our ill passenger was on the road to recovery.

Jean stayed with me as we continued to watch over our German patient next to the cockpit. She allowed me to sit in one of the cabin crew chairs up front as the plane began the approach to the destination airport. About twenty minutes later, Flight 924 landed uneventfully at Lindbergh Field in San Diego a little after midnight.

After the large front door of the 767 opened, paramedics rushed in and put Greta on a stretcher. I briefed them on her vital signs and medical condition and gave them my name and cell phone number just in case.

Max was beside himself with tears of joy. I wished him and Greta the best, and they shook my hand in gratitude.

"*Viel Glück in allem!*" they said (Good luck in everything) as they were taken to the paramedics truck.

Still near the cockpit, Jean and I waited for the sleepy passengers to file out of the plane.

Some smiles and thanks came our way, in appreciation for the efforts that helped our fellow passenger.

Not seeing Sienna, I walked to the middle of the airliner and found her waiting with our bags ready. She gave me a big hug and told me what she had heard from the grapevine. There were some obvious inaccuracies (for example, Greta did NOT have a heart attack and she did NOT receive an electrical shock from a defibrillator) but the other details were on the money.

Sienna felt she missed out on some major drama during the flight and that I was some sort of a hero now. To downplay the whole hero thing, I nonchalantly said, "Just another day at the office. Only 30,000 feet up!"

To me, it was all about staying upbeat and helping in a situation with the available tools at hand. And I could not have been as effective if the flight attendants had not been so cooperative and professional.

After Sienna and I deplaned and then arrived at the terminal gate, an airline official named Charles shook my hand and said he needed to discuss some details of the in-flight events for a few minutes if I did not mind. I agreed to the meeting, and Sienna went to freshen up in the ladies' room.

The man was a representative of the airline and had been told of the medical flight emergency. He asked me if I felt there was enough support by the airline staff while I cared for the passenger on board.

"Definitely!" I answered. "They helped me quite a bit and did all they could to assist on behalf of the sick passenger."

He was glad to hear my words.

I asked Charles, "I wonder... is there a standard medical kit used on all flights?"

The airline rep told me it was standard to have two kits on board: one for standard first aid, the other intended for more severe medical emergencies.

"You know," he continued, "there are no universal guidelines on what to do during in-flight medical emergencies."

"Most of the time," Charles said, "the flight attendants can handle the problem. But they rely on willing off-duty medical professionals on board to provide appropriate assistance when needed and when possible."

Charles went on to say that sometimes doctors on a flight fail to offer aid because of possible liability issues. He reassured me that any doctor providing medical assistance in good faith on a domestic flight is protected under the Good Samaritan laws in this country. In 1998, the U.S. passed the Aviation Medical Assistance Act, which includes a Good Samaritan provision.

In recognition of my efforts on behalf of Greta, I was given a voucher good for any round-trip domestic flight on the airline, up to a certain dollar value. I expressed my appreciation to the airline official and caught up with Sienna.

"What did the man have to say?" she asked, not able to hide her sleepiness.

"Oh, he just wanted to clarify some particulars on the in-flight events," I replied.

The news about the voucher could wait until the next day, I thought.

We slowly walked through the almost empty airport, heading to the baggage claim area. It was almost 1 a.m. after a long travel day, and all Sienna could talk about was falling asleep in her bed.

I, on the other hand, was wide awake because of the dramatic happenings on Flight 924. I felt a great sense of satisfaction realizing that the efforts of the cabin crew and myself were rewarded with Greta's clearly improved health. At the same time, I was at one with the world as I thought back on my unexpected "house call" on this vacation night flight.

Landing in Lindbergh Field,

San Diego, California

CHAPTER IV: Taking the Bull by the Horns

The spectacle of bullfighting, which is also known as *tauromachia*, is often linked to Rome, where many human-versus-animal "sports" were held in the grand Colosseum. This controversial pastime is now still popular in the Iberian Peninsula and some Latin American countries. Protesters point out the clear suffering of the bulls for the sake of entertainment, but those who espouse the institution claim it is an art form deeply rooted in many cultures and traditions.

Before the matadors and their assistants can fight the bulls in the ring, however, these huge animals must first be taken to the arena. Centuries ago, to get the beasts from the corrals which were some distance from the bullring, town drovers would simply herd the bulls to the stadium. Over time, some of the butchers (having the responsibility of buying the bulls) began to join the herders to guide the animals to the bullring.

Eventually, by the 14th or 15th century, others began to run *in front of* the bulls (not behind them as the drovers and butchers did) as a show of bravado and in the spirit of competition. The declared winner was able to get the bulls to the bullfighting arena more quickly.

Initially, only a few intrepid souls dared to risk injury with such a display of bull running. Due to a curious phenomenon, though, this dangerous activity has attracted more and more participants with the passage of time. Now, various celebrations around the globe highlight this once obscure practice.

Ernest Hemingway's classic 1926 novel *The Sun Also Rises* described the festival of San Fermín and its pièce de résistance, El Encierro (Spanish for the Running of the Bulls). This world-famous extravaganza is the largest display of bull running on the planet, and it is held annually from July 7th to July 14th in the small quaint town of Pamplona, Spain.

I had traveled to Spain several years ago with my mother and brother Ron, exploring areas such as Madrid, Granada, Sevilla, and the Costa del

Sol. Due to personal matters, my brother Manny was unable to join us, and he regretted not making the trip.

Around the time of Memorial Day a few years back, I brought up the idea of a trip to Europe with Manny. He was instantly on board, and we agreed that Spain would be on the itinerary. Knowing my adventurous demeanor, Manny realized that revisiting the same regions in Spain (as I had in the past) was not under consideration.

La Tomatina, a festival held in August in the municipality of Buñol, Spain, was brought up by my brother. The highlight of the celebration is a tomato fight that lasts from 11 a.m. to 12 p.m., with the tomatoes having to be squashed before thrown and no other projectiles allowed. And before the tomato launching begins, the *palo jabón* event takes place, during which someone must successfully climb a greasy pole and knock down a ham situated at the top.

I liked Manny's idea, but something more sensational was on my mind. It did not take long before I suggested the possibility of El Encierro in the small city of Pamplona, Spain. This famous event was mentioned by my friend Melanie just before the Memorial Day weekend since she knew of some guys who had traveled to this spectacle the year before. To me, it was not a coincidence that she decided to tell me about her story at that specific time.

Manny was not immediately enthusiastic about the idea of bull running, but he was more than willing to at least visit the town during the famous jamboree. To add to the appeal of the trip, I also suggested a few days in nearby Barcelona before the gest in Pamplona. In no time, my brother agreed to join me in the ambitious excursion. We also concurred that I would spearhead the preparations for the adventure less than six weeks away.

The fiesta of San Fermín (known as Los Sanfermines in Spain) honors St. Fermín, the saint of bakers and wine merchants. He was the first bishop of Pamplona and gained martyrdom in the Catholic Church when he was beheaded in Amiens, France, in 303 A.D. Another less popular story claims that he met his death by being dragged through the streets of Pamplona by bulls.

Owing to time-honored tradition, residents of Pamplona and tourists who don't want to stick out like a sore thumb wear white clothing and red kerchiefs around their necks during the jubilee.

The red neckerchief or scarf is definitely symbolic of the blood of St. Fermín, who was probably decapitated at Amiens. On the other hand, there is no clear consensus as to why the garb is mostly-white, although the Spanish people point out that the color white clearly stands out in a crowd.

After the Fourth of July weekend in America, Manny and I had a feeling of great anticipation as we made final preparations for the upcoming Spanish vacation. We decided to purchase our white pants and shirts and red kerchiefs before the trip. Each of us also bought the optional red sash to wear around the waist. Before we knew it, it was time to board our flight to the Iberian Peninsula.

We brushed up on our Spanish as we flew across the United States and then the Atlantic Ocean. Barcelona, located on the northeast coast of Spain, would be our first stop, and a few days later we would be off to Pamplona, about 300 miles due northwest near the border with France. I was fairly certain that I would be running with the bulls, but Manny had yet to decide. Maybe he would become inspired once we set foot on Spanish soil.

In the modern city of Barcelona, host to the 1992 Summer Olympics and the second largest city in Spain, we had a grand time. The people were friendly and the lifestyle was active. And our sightseeing included the towering Sagrada Família cathedral (still under construction), the Arc de Triomf with colorful brickwork, and the distinctive Torre Agbar (the bullet-shaped tower, especially spectacular when illuminated at night).

The few days in this growing city with the Mediterranean climate were uplifting and clearly refreshing. In addition, the parks and promenades and beaches were perfect for exploring and getting to know the locals.

Soon, though, the main focus of our vacation would be upon us.

On a Wednesday morning, we checked out of our hotel and headed for Barcelona-El Prat Airport, the second largest in Spain. We went through the usual security checkpoints before waiting for our Iberia Airlines flight with destination Pamplona. After a short journey, the small aircraft touched down in Pamplona, the capital of the Navarra region of Northern Spain.

A taxi took us to our hotel just south of the city. After unloading our luggage, we sauntered into a nearby restaurant for some *tapas* (appetizers) and sangria. Locals and tourists at the eatery were clearly in a cheerful mood as the San Fermín festival was already under way. As we imbibed our drinks, we were told that the celebrations had begun about three days prior. More importantly, Manny and I found out that the Running of the Bulls would take place daily at 8 a.m. for eight days during the fiesta.

The sun the following morning was brilliant, and we set off by foot into Pamplona. The town was founded by Pompey as a military settlement in 75 B.C. And as we approached the city, we discovered that the old walls and fortifications were still prominent.

When we reached the Plaza del Castillo, it was a sight to see virtually everyone sporting the white outfits with red neckerchiefs (*pañuelos*) that we were wearing. This large square is the nerve center of Pamplona and is the site where the city's former castle once stood.

A band played vibrant Spanish music and most onlookers were in a jovial mood, at least partly due to the alcohol consumed with vitality. No police force was seen, but no drunken violence was apparent either. We walked down the adjacent local streets and all stores and bars were overflowing with tourists and native Spaniards alike.

Taking in some libations at a crowded tavern, I made small talk with two amicable *señoritas* who were there on vacation from Southern Spain. They were looking forward to watching El Encierro but had no intention of running with the bulls, despite my best efforts to inveigle them.

Later on, as we gazed at the interesting façade of an antique shop, Manny and I were greeted by a small group of vocal and mildly tipsy Pamplona residents. They took a photo with us, correctly deduced that we were just visiting, and welcomed us to their town. This encounter epitomized a carefree friendliness that suffused the entire scene.

I saw some exotic items in the local shops, but a T-shirt caught my eye. This piece of clothing was covered front and back with a black-and-white image of sheer pandemonium. It showed several black bulls chasing dozens of men dressed in mostly-white shirts and pants. Just then, my pulse rose in anticipation of the next day. Soon enough, the novelty item was on the checkout counter as I paid in euros.

After visiting our second or third watering hole, my brother and I walked some more around the historic city. There were old buildings several stories high with elegant predominantly-green banners or tapestry hung from the balconies. A parade was in progress, with characters including Gigantes y Cabezudos (Giants and Big-Heads), partly representing past kings and queens. And some exhibition sports, including stone lifting and wood cutting, were on display.

Many streets were packed with hundreds of men, women, and children, circulating in a town of only nine square miles. People would often join the loud parades, in which many played drums and trumpets and carried flags. Men in traditional black and red uniforms rode well-trained horses, while the spectators wore the ubiquitous white garb with red *pañuelos* and sashes.

After enjoying the festivities for a few hours, Manny and I knew it was time to scope out the route that I (and possibly he) would be navigating in less than 24 hours.

The path of the bulls during the *encierro* (bull run) starts in the walled-off stall where six large bulls and six to eight large oxen (castrated male cattle) are kept. At 8 a.m. sharp, the doors of the corral are thrown open to release several oxen onto the streets of Pamplona. Seconds later, the six bulls are let go to follow the oxen. Less than 30 seconds later, two or three more oxen are let out to follow the bulls. All these hefty animals follow a predetermined route that is walled off by buildings or wooden barricades constructed for the event.

The entire distance covered by the bulls and oxen is a little over 900 yards, ending in the Plaza de Toros arena for the bullfighting soon to follow. It will take these 1500-2000+ pound animals only about two minutes to travel the entire course.

The brave (or crazy – you decide) fellows and few ladies who choose to participate in El Encierro actually do not line the entire path of the bulls. We humans are allowed to begin our run about 100 yards from the corral of the bulls. So participants have a head start, at least for a while.

At the outset of our run, there is the mild incline of the relatively narrow Calle de Santo Domingo, which is enclosed by stone buildings and walls. There is no place for runners to take refuge in this initial section, and the bulls are full of energy. Consequently, this stretch is the most dangerous part of the run to start from.

Afterwards, participants enter El Plaza Consistorial (Town Hall Square), in front of

Ayuntamiento de Pamplona (Town Hall). There, bulls and runners have more room to spread out, with wooden barricades in place (and spaces between the barriers serving as escape points for some people). At the end of the square, animals and humans go through a small street named Mercaderes and make a sharp right turn to prepare for the next section.

After Mercaderes lies the narrow street called Calle de la Estafeta, which is lined with businesses and shops. If needed, one can get out of the way of the charging bulls in this area by moving into the niches at the entrances of the stores. Still, the tightness of the straightaway street increases the chances of contact with a bull.

If one is still on his or her feet, there is the final stretch of Telefónica, a narrow path of 100 yards, and Callejón, a short corridor with downhill slope leading to the bullring. The animals may speed up here, and the narrow path leads to potential pile-ups of participants.

The runner who makes it to the bullfighting arena needs to be wary of the sandy ground, which can cause the not-so-nimble person to fall. He or she then becomes an easier target for an angry bull.

Knowing the aforementioned layout of the Running of the Bulls, each of the 2500 or so running participants on a given day can choose his/her strategy regarding where to be positioned once the bulls are released. This decision usually determines the degree of risk accepted.

The most confident daredevils place themselves at the human starting line – a little under 100 yards from the corral. They encounter the raging bulls first and run in between and alongside them with caution. The next most courageous begin their experience farther up the Calle de Santo Domingo, at varying distances from the start line, still with no escape points to avoid a rampaging bull.

Those wishing to take less risk begin in the town hall square, which is an open space with points of exit between the barricades. Calle de la Estafeta, the longest part of the course, can be relatively safe for the participants, with areas of refuge at store entrances, provided they avoid colliding with other runners in this narrow street.

Manny and I marched through the entire 900 yards of the path that would be dominated by fighting bulls in the *encierro* event. In the course of our tour of the bull run route, I succeeded in persuading him to join me in running with the bulls the next day. The whole time, I predicted that once he was exposed to the festive environment, he was sure to get into the spirit of the celebrations, and bull running was an essential part of the experience.

Sunset was approaching, so we headed back to our hotel to get some food and important rest. Because of the vacation atmosphere and despite the excitement level, our sleep was surprisingly good. Upon arising the next day, we knew that the following hours would be among the most memorable in our lives.

Once again wearing our festival white garments with red neckerchiefs and sashes, Manny and I took a cab to the center of Pamplona. Thousands of people were already in a party atmosphere as we arrived at the route of El Encierro.

Initially, we thought about being conservative and planting ourselves in El Plaza Consistorial. This plan was sensible and probably involved the least peril. Of course, there was always the chance that another participant runs into you and causes you to fall, leaving you vulnerable to being trampled by the fast behemoths.

We were hopeful that all the runners in the bull run were alert and agile. Alas, that was not the case. There were still some participants who were somewhat inebriated from the night before, posing an extra risk to themselves and other people. The police officers were very watchful, though, and before the *encierro* began, Manny and I saw several prospective runners being removed from the scene because of suspected intoxication.

As the 8 a.m. start time neared, Manny headed to the town hall area as planned. But I was not so sure.

In my mind, I knew that I would regret my decision if I did not at least consider starting my run in the precarious uphill Calle de Santo Domingo. Who knows if I would have this opportunity again. And I thought to myself that I was fairly fast on my feet. In times like these, we all must choose what is "best" in the long run, so those I-should-have-done-that moments do not surface in the future.

There are occasions when a cautious approach is called for. But this was not one of those times for me.

At about 7:45 a.m., I told Manny of my decision to begin my run in the initial dangerous uphill portion, joining the risk takers on Calle de Santo Domingo. He felt somewhat better when I decided to position myself not at the starting line for the runners, but about 50 yards away. At that vantage point, I would be able to see the front runners make their moves as the bulls first approached.

We high-fived each other and shouted, "What a rush!"

Our plan was to eventually meet at the Plaza de Toros (bullfighting arena) following the arrival of all the bulls. I walked toward Santo Domingo, invigorated, knowing that I had made the right decision.

My first reaction upon arriving at my chosen starting point was surprise at how close together my fellow participants stood. People were almost shoulder-to-shoulder in some areas. As the time of reckoning approached, some runners calmly read the local newspaper or talked to other runners. At the other extreme, a few were loquacious and very animated, displaying a braggadocio about the upcoming event.

Minutes before 8 a.m., everyone around me began to walk toward an area near the human starting line. They were gathering around a stone enclave about ten feet high, approximately ten yards from where the front runners would begin their sprint. A small statue of San Fermín was on display there, along with 17 decorative pieces of cloth. Of these, 15 commemorated a gruesome past.

In the history of El Encierro, over 200 people per year in the course of the eight bull runs suffer minor injuries, due to collisions and falls and relatively mild trauma inflicted by the massive bulls. They live to fight another day. However, since records have been kept, a total of 15 people (all men) have died due to participation in the popular extravaganza. All but two (one Mexican, one American) of the deaths have been Spaniards, and all 15 are memorialized before each bull run.

It is tradition that in the several minutes before each *encierro*, all the participant runners hold a rolled-up local newspaper and raise it toward the statue of San Fermín, moving it to and fro. At that time, he/she sings or says the following oath of San Fermín:

"*A San Fermín pedimos, por ser nuestro patrón, nos guíe en el encierro dándonos su bendición. Viva San Fermín! Gora San Fermín*!" (We ask St. Fermín, our patron saint, to guide us through the bull run and give us his blessing. Long live St. Fermín!)

The chant is done three times in the five minutes before the bulls are released from the corrals. Before and after each mantra, there is almost pure silence in the midst of the upcoming frenzy. As a prelude to the bull run, the oath is almost mesmerizing to some.

As an international event that attracts thousands of spectators each year, El Encierro has its share of media coverage. I saw two national television correspondents and several local news reporters near the starting line interviewing various participants. Excitement and some fear were probably apparent as I told one newsperson that it was my first time. She and her crew were impressed by my willingness to join in their local festival. In my mind, I imagined that the Spanish viewers on TV thought this American newbie was in over his head.

In the minutes before the start, I sensed the trepidation in the air. As I moved toward the point from which I would begin my run, I met an Italian 30-something who was a dead ringer for Jessica Alba.

Valeria was also in Pamplona for the first time and like me opted to start in the more challenging first part of the route. Her strategy was to begin about halfway up Calle de Santo Domingo, wait for the rushing bulls to appear around the corner, then run ahead of the animals for a short distance before escaping between barricades in the town hall square.

As we talked, I saw that she was a little anxious. To lessen the pre-run tension, in my best Ray Lewis impression, I uttered, "Let's do this!"

She forced out a grin.

Recent statistics have shown that over half of those running with the bulls are first-timers, and that only about five percent are women. From my view, Valeria was the sole lady on Santo Domingo. I commended her for her bravery.

Suddenly, a small rocket was shot into the sky, and I glimpsed my watch which indicated 8 a.m. When I asked my new Italian acquaintance the meaning of the launch, she said the gate to the corral had just been opened to release the first oxen and then the six bulls. Less than 15 seconds later, a second rocket was shot, meaning the second set of oxen had left the corral.

It was now only a matter of seconds before the enormous creatures would be in our sights (the path between the corral and the human starting line was around the corner and not visible to us). Valeria quickly moved up the street toward her planned start area while I stayed put, about 50 yards from the front runners.

"Best of luck!" she told me.

Most of the participants around me seemed alert and apprehensive, but one or two appeared a little preoccupied. I remembered then that many of the people injured each year owe their misfortunes to nearby runners who either ran into them or fell down in their paths and tripped them up. As much as possible, it was my goal to keep my distance from my fellow thrill-seekers.

I spotted the first oxen and bulls racing around the corner to reach the courageous front runners. These beasts were larger-than-life, with the average bull weighing a ton or more. The oxen, castrated and less aggressive, were just as huge, with bells hanging around their necks. At that surreal moment, I momentarily could not move, taking in the scene of imminent danger.

My adrenaline level rose further as I saw a blurry horde of men in white and red rushing toward me and ahead of the bovine onslaught. Several participants were moving alongside the fierce beasts, even trying to touch them, in various degrees of bravado. Most were staying at least a few feet away from the massive creatures. Instinctively, my body and legs began to move, trying to dodge other men as the bulls approached. Within seconds, these powerful animals were about 10 yards from me.

In the midst of this frenzied backdrop, I concentrated on staying at least five or ten yards ahead of or away from the charging bulls and oxen, choosing to run to their left. Going up the mild incline of Calle de Santo Domingo, my pace was surprisingly maintained ahead of the leviathans. A fellow participant ran in my path and almost tripped me, but I managed to remain on my feet.

As the bulls and I approached El Plaza Consistorial, a male runner about five yards ahead fell down as he lost his balance while avoiding another man. One of the oxen stomped on his arm and back.

The town hall square was now in view, and I saw Valeria slip through an opening between wooden barriers to safety. I, on the other hand, was not yet in the clear.

The rambunctious beasts were now more spread out in the square. Losing ground to them, I veered further to the bulls' left and ran beside one and then another. I was momentarily tempted to try to touch one as it passed me, but my better judgment set in. A few bulls and oxen rapidly moved past me, and the roar of the herd still remains vivid to this day.

In El Plaza Consistorial, many called it a day and left the course between the wooden barricades. The majority, though, chose to continue on and complete the entire bull run. My energy level was still quite high, and a naïve confidence pushed me forward.

At the far end of the town square lies the short street Mercaderes, where the *encierro* course takes an abrupt right turn. Invariably, some bulls and oxen each year cannot manage the sudden change in direction and end up ramming into the barricade to their left.

I was about five yards behind when two bulls and one ox slid into the wooden barrier before continuing their rush down Calle de la Estafeta. As the animals hit the rampart, a few runners barely escaped being crushed by the behemoths. A few days later, I would find out that one of the eight bull runs that year involved human injuries at this dangerous bend.

Arriving at the straight and narrow Calle de la Estafeta, I saw the creatures bunched up once again. Many men and women had taken their places at the safe entryways of businesses lining the street. Some of them were squabbling over certain spots.

By this time, I was trailing the majority of bulls by almost ten yards, while two or three oxen dashed past me. This second set of oxen was let go after the bulls to guide or encourage the bulls toward the bullring. Despite the relatively slower pace in this latter part of the run, a few people still fell down as a result of frantic pushing and shoving in a confined space.

On average, it takes the average person less than four minutes to complete the entire *encierro* route, which ends at the Plaza de Toros. To the novice who intends to make it to the finish, there is still the prospect of the Curva de Telefónica, a sharp bend in the short path between Calle de la Estafeta and the bullring. At this potential disaster zone, human pile-ups have occurred as the bulls are led into the arena building itself.

Once all the gargantuan animals are safely in the bullring, the large doors are closed. Inside, there are thousands of spectators already in the stands, along with participant runners who ran with the bulls. Later in the day, there will be the bullfighting finale for the six unlucky bulls.

I was not able to enter the bullfighting arena before the doors were shut. A rocket blast (the third of the morning) sounded, signifying that all bulls and oxen had reached the ring. Minutes later, a fourth and final rocket was fired, meaning all animals had been successfully contained in the Plaza de Toros corrals.

Manny completed his run without a scratch and managed to enter the arena afterwards. He later told me he had the chance to take some photographs of the festivities in the bull ring. Reportedly, the bulls and oxen were moving haphazardly around the center area, with many people also flitting about in harm's way.

Fortunately, *dobladores* (dressed in green shirts) kept the order. These skilled professionals, some ex-bullfighters, steered the animals to safe areas in the arena by using capes to distract them. In addition, the *dobladores* promoted the safety of the runners still left in the ring.

El Encierro is not for everyone, and it is not even for most people. You need to be physically fit, fast on your feet, and cool-minded. And it is important to know that rules do not allow a participant to simply stay in one spot and watch the bulls and runners pass. In other words, he/she must be *running with the bulls*.

Many onlookers attend this celebrated event yearly, lining the periphery of the route or safely relaxing in balconies or areas overlooking the path. In the past, being on the periphery did not guarantee safety, though. One spectator was killed when a bull managed to get past a wooden barrier. Thanks to double rows of fencing now used, such disasters are avoided.

The fiesta of San Fermín has clearly been highlighted by the world-famous Running of the Bulls year in and year out. This showpiece of the festival is a highly risky exploit, defined by the dangers accepted by participant runners and the mettle and physical abilities displayed by them. When one considers the entire scenario, this event may actually be unimaginable in any other place in the world.

But if you are looking for a once-in-a-lifetime experience between the 7th and 14th of July, think about heading to Northern Spain in your white and red. And consider it the ultimate incentive to improve your foot speed.

Pamplona, Spain

CHAPTER V: Vacation Interrupted

October 10th 2010. Or 10-10-10. A very significant date for all those numerologists out there. And for yours truly, a birthday to boot.

Over coffee at our favorite bistro, my girlfriend Sienna and I talked about what we might do to make that distinctive day that much more special. In the course of an hour, dozens of unusual suggestions came up, from visiting the 10th U.S. state (that's Virginia, if you're trying out for *Jeopardy*!) to hiking Mount McKinley (the tallest peak in the United States) to vacationing in Longyearbyen, Norway (site of the world's northernmost permanent airport).

As our conversation continued, I set my sights ever so high, picturing a trip to the tallest building in the world, on the other side of the globe. That would be the Burj Khalifa, formerly known as the

Burj Dubai, in the United Arab Emirates (U.A.E.) city of Dubai.

Yes, there would be some possible danger, given the volatile state of the Middle East. And clothing restrictions were to be expected, especially for Sienna, in this Muslim country. Furthermore, we would want to learn at least some basic Arabic in a relatively short period of time.

On the other side of the coin, an excursion to Dubai should be quite remarkable. We would get a view of the world from the tallest skyscraper on Earth, the Burj Khalifa, towering at 2722 feet and boasting the most floors of any building (163) and the fastest elevator on the planet (reaching speeds of 40 miles per hour).

The extravagant Burj Al Arab, shaped like the sail of a ship and the world's only "7-star hotel" (officially a 5-Star Deluxe hotel), would be one of our stops. And we could behold the Dubai Fountain, the world's largest and tallest musical fountain project, offering spectacular daily performances set to music and light.

In the course of a few lunches and dinners, Sienna and I chatted about the prospect of traveling halfway around the planet to the exotic destination. Neither of us had ever been to the

Arabian Peninsula, and none of our friends had ever visited that part of the globe. Was it as hot as people said? What customs would we have to familiarize ourselves with? Would it be safe?

We did some research and talked over the logistics of such a long journey. In time, the allure of Dubai won out over any possible drawbacks. The date of the adventure, 10-10-10, was already established. What remained was the planning for the many other details of this unusual trip.

Sienna and I sought the best price online for getting to Dubai and discovered that the most economical itinerary involved a stopover in the Xarantine International Airport in Xarantine City, the nation's capital (names have been changed for privacy reasons). However, perusing internet sites on airport reviews, we found several complaints about this facility. Mention was made of unhelpful and rude staff, long walks between terminals, delays at the passport control areas, and very expensive food. To be fair, other travelers' comments were favorable or at least lukewarm.

My girlfriend thought out loud, "How bad could it be? The stopover there is only an hour or two, and the long walks would be a good way to stretch our legs."

I agreed with my bold travel companion. If we could save several hundred dollars with this layover in Xarantine, a little inconvenience was worth it.

Once we looked at our work schedules, Sienna and I saw eye to eye on the travel plans that would put us in Dubai by October 10th. A short flight from San Diego to Los Angeles would be followed by a transcontinental journey to JFK International Airport in Queens, New York. From there, a voyage across the Atlantic Ocean and Europe would end in Xarantine City. Following a two-hour stopover at the Xarantine International Airport, a final flight would last a few hours before we arrived in the U.A.E. If plans proceeded as scheduled, we would touch down at the Dubai International Airport on October 9th.

After some practical decisions were made on accommodations in Dubai, we finalized the airline ticket purchases and hotel reservations. My girlfriend and I also learned some basic Arabic phrases and words, and we packed appropriate clothing for the climate and culture. Everything seemed to be going swimmingly.

On an October afternoon, I found myself in line with Sienna at Lindbergh Field airport in San Diego, California, as our exotic adventure began.

The one-hour flight to Los Angeles went without a hitch, and our LAX layover would only last about two hours. Some sculptures and origami by local artists were on display and the airport was hectic as usual. We did some people watching, hoping to catch a celebrity or two. Looking at the monitors, we saw that the flight on United Airlines to New York City was on time.

Boarding the airliner bound for JFK, we coincidentally met a young couple from Trenton, New Jersey, who had been to Xarantine City and specifically to the Xarantine International Airport. They related a fairly good experience when they stopped at that airport on vacation two years prior en route to New Delhi, India. Maybe those complainers on the internet were the outliers.

After takeoff, Sienna and I stared through our window at the downtown Los Angeles skyline. Once in the air at cruising altitude, I gazed in wonder at the flight information available at my fingertips on the small view screen. External temperature: -60 degrees Fahrenheit. Equivalent ground speed of the aircraft: 550 miles per hour. Altitude: 36,000 feet. And here I was sitting comfortably on a reclining chair.

Most of our transcontinental voyage was pleasant, save for some intermittent turbulence and a haughty passenger who felt he deserved special attention. He was quickly scolded by a stern flight attendant. A perfect landing on the tarmac ended our flight from the City of Angels to The City That Never Sleeps.

With the time change, it was almost 2 a.m. in New York City. Once in the bright airport terminal, we looked at the flight schedule monitors and found the gate number for the intercontinental flight that was still a few hours away. Stores and restaurants were all closed, and I purchased some food and drink from the vending machines.

After our snack, Sienna and I found a comfortable area where we could lie down and sleep for a few hours. Around 5:30 a.m., we awoke and waited for a restaurant to open. For breakfast, we took down some pancakes and omelets before heading to the airline gate. The scheduled flight to Xarantine City was to leave at 7 a.m., but the gate attendant informed us of a mild delay in our journey to the capital of Xarantine. She tried to reassure us that we should still make our connection to Dubai at the airport.

We smiled at the helpful lady and began to take a walk around the airport terminal. It was daybreak in the Big Apple as we looked through the large airport windows. Minutes later, rain drops were hitting the glass.

About 30 minutes before the updated flight time, passengers were arriving at the gate area. Everyone seemed calm and patient. Some asked the gate attendants about possible seating changes. Elsewhere, a child was sleeping in her mother's lap. I saw a man in a business suit reading the *Wall Street Journal*.

Soon, it was 15 minutes before flight time, and rain was now loudly pounding on the airport terminal windows. The news on the TV monitors described a local storm brewing, and the word "DELAYED" was posted next to various flights on the display monitors. Our flight was officially moved back an additional hour.

We overheard some disgruntled passengers commenting on the untoward weather, but Sienna and I remained optimistic that the flight delay would not drastically alter our scheduled itinerary. After we talked about the situation with the gate attendant, however, our hopes were dashed.

It was revealed that the updated departure time at JFK would not allow us to make our planned connection flight at Xarantine City going to Dubai. Instead, once we arrived at Xarantine International Airport, we would have no choice but to take the next scheduled plane to the U.A.E. – 12 hours after the original time. My girlfriend and I inquired about any available alternative flights from JFK to Dubai International at that time, but none was offered. Sienna sighed.

Eventually, the rain died down and our impatient fellow travelers joined us at the airline gate. We all boarded the aircraft in a generally orderly fashion. Apologies were expressed by the various airline staff, and Sienna and I settled into our seats, thinking about how we could pass the time for 12 hours at the airport in Xarantine City.

During the transatlantic trip, after a small meal was served, I looked at my personal in-flight entertainment screen and discovered a game called Cranium (or a name similar to that). This diversion gave me trivia questions on sundry topics (geography, movies, history, etc.) together with a multiple choice format for the possible answers.

What surprised me was that all passengers (identified by seat number and chosen moniker) playing the trivia game at the same time were being scored for all to see. As a result, a friendly competition developed during the flight. The winner of each 20-question game was announced on the screen, and he/she had bragging rights, at least until the next game. Enjoying the challenge, I was able to prevail in several of the contests.

The hours passed quickly on the flight. My girlfriend and I reviewed some basic Arabic, the official language in Dubai, from our travel book. After playing my umpteenth game of Cranium, I heard an overhead tone. Soon after, the main flight attendant announced in three different languages the upcoming descent toward the Xarantine International Airport.

Following a fairly smooth touchdown onto the runway, the large Boeing 767 airliner reached the international terminal. After disembarking from the jet and entering the arrivals gate, Sienna and I sought an information desk. Our originally scheduled connection flight from Xarantine City to Dubai had in fact departed over an hour prior due to our delay from JFK.

Others were also affected by the aforementioned flight changes, and we were all directed to a booth bombarded with many passengers in disarray. Some semblance of a queue eventually formed, and we waited in line with some impatience.

After half an hour, we reached the front of the line. The two of us showed the welcoming agent our passports and inquired about the next available flight to Dubai. As we had expected, it was over 10 hours away.

When Sienna asked what our options were for the long layover in Xarantine City, the airport employee gave us two choices. Option number one involved us passing the time in the almost deserted airport terminal overnight (it was almost 3 a.m. local time), with no stores or food places open for hours. Sienna did not favor this proposal, so option number two instantly won out.

We would be staying in a *transit hotel* overnight, with expenses paid by the airline. This type of short-stay accommodation is usually located in an airport that is a busy transfer hub, within security checkpoints. And even though we did not have visas for Xarantine, Sienna and I could stay at said hotel without having to clear the immigration control section of the airport. Not common in the United States, these hotels are most prevalent in Asia and parts of Europe.

"That doesn't sound so bad," I said, and my girlfriend agreed.

The professional but serious airport officials told us to wait for a shuttle to the hotel, and it arrived about 15 minutes later. In the interim, three other couples had joined us. Soon, we all discovered that this transit hotel was not on airport grounds.

All eight of us were greeted by the shuttle driver and his assistant and they inspected our passports. We were led through the electronic glass doors and experienced the cold Xarantine night. A small shuttle vehicle awaited us, and we were then driven through a dark part of the airport toward a sentry station.

At the gate, a guard with a rifle looked at some papers supplied by the driver's assistant. He was satisfied and the gate opened to let us out of the airport grounds. The shuttle was driven onto the local highway and we gazed at the lighted signs and the few other cars on the road. An uneasy silence permeated the air.

Within minutes, we exited the highway and headed toward an 8-story Best Eastern Hotel (not its real name). The eight of us were directed off the vehicle and led to the hotel lobby. No other guests were seen at this early morning hour. Without saying another word, our airport escorts left us at the check-in desk.

The hotel staff appeared and told us that our brief stay at the Best Eastern would be in the transit hotel section. There were two people allowed per room, with all rooms located on a certain wing of the fifth floor. In addition, a breakfast would be provided for each chamber. Finally, we were only allowed to make telephone calls within the hotel during our sojourn.

Two bellhops took the eight of us up the elevator to the fifth floor. We reached the transit hotel section, and more restrictions were announced.

We were not allowed to leave this designated section of the hotel until our trip back to the airport. Only our assigned rooms and adjacent hallway were authorized areas. There was to be no communication between the occupants of different chambers. And a guard would be at the entrance/exit point of the transit hotel section and hallway.

Two of the eight tourists in the group, Joe and Betty, a couple from Upstate New York, objected to these strict rules. They thought their rights were being violated. To these complainers, Torin (the guard or watchman) said they were free to return to the airport and stay there overnight instead. The duo thought for a minute before agreeing to the conditions of their stay.

To me, it was reasonable for the Xarantine government to take these precautions involving international travelers who had no visa to stay in the country. Sienna and I chose not to obtain visas since we had planned on being in Xarantine City for only one or two hours during an airport stopover. Unless one gets an invitation from a Xarantine citizen or company, obtaining a tourist visa to Xarantine usually entails going through a visa service or visa expediting agency. The document is finally issued at an embassy or consulate. Such a process can take weeks and cost up to a few hundred dollars.

The three other couples, Sienna, and I were directed to our rooms, which I recall being somewhat spartan. My girlfriend turned on the television, which mostly featured shows in the Xarantine language. The radio did not work. We decided to call the front desk to request a wake-up call in the morning and give our preferences for breakfast.

For the next eight or nine hours, this small chamber and the adjacent hallway would be our humble abode. We did have a view through our room's window of the fairly classy lobby four floors below, but all restaurants and shops were closed. I went out to the hallway to stretch my legs, only to have our guard encourage me to return to my room. Jokingly, I thought to myself:

I guess an early morning stroll in the lobby with my girlfriend was out of the question.

Sienna and I tried to ride with the punches. But she eventually began to feel a little claustrophobic. I tried to calm her down, but she was compelled to take a walk. I accompanied her into the hallway, but within a few minutes, we were told by Torin to retreat to our room.

Suddenly, being tired and antsy, she started yelling at the man, blaming him for the rules we were supposed to follow and asking who was responsible for these restrictions in the first place. In response, Torin warned Sienna that her loud voice and lack of cooperation may lead to unfortunate consequences.

In time, she lowered her voice, and I managed to convince my girlfriend to get back into our chamber. We ate some protein bars I had stashed in my luggage and played some cards before falling asleep.

In what seemed like a minute or two later, we were awakened by some shouting that was coming from the hallway. After jumping out of bed, we opened the door and caught sight of quite a scene. Two men in dark blue-green uniforms and matching hats were trying to detain a middle-aged bearded man and a brunette, both in their pajamas.

The uniformed men were armed – we saw their holsters and pistols – but they did not reach for their weapons. They were silent as the civilian couple shouted in English and some French.

I overheard the lady saying, "*Otez vos mains de moi!*" (Take your hands off of me!).

In the scuffle, the bearded transit hotel guest pushed the slimmer but taller armed man, who lost his balance and fell to the ground. Instantly, he unstrapped his holster and drew his gun. His partner then pulled out his pistol as well, with both pistols now pointed at the two hotel guests.

The lady and her male friend put their hands up and backed down. He then said in perfect English, "No need for violence. We'll come quietly."

The taller officer got up on his feet and put away his gun. His partner continued to point his pistol at the couple, who were then put in plastic handcuffs. As they were led down the hallway and out of the transit hotel, the couple under arrest looked dejected as their heads drooped forward.

By this time, about seven doors were open in the hallway, all but one with onlookers in quiet disbelief. Torin appeared and instructed all of us to get back to sleep. We asked for an explanation but none was given. No one decided to push the issue as we all walked back to our rooms.

Sienna and I pondered the possible reasons why two travelers would be taken away by uniformed men in the middle of the night. Smuggling? Terrorism? Espionage? We knew it was not for complaining about our temporary accommodations, since Joe and Betty were not the ones arrested and Sienna was still with me.

After about 20 minutes, I elected to calmly approach our night watchman. I asked if he could tell me anything about what had just happened.

Torin said nothing for about 30 seconds before mumbling, "They were removed for being in violation of Xarantine law."

Nothing more specific was revealed, and he urged me to ask no more questions for my own good.

Not surprisingly, back in our modest room, Sienna and I found it difficult to get back to sleep after the incident. Would there be someone knocking on *our* door soon? Was I asking our guard too many questions? Did Sienna shout too loudly at Torin earlier that night? We took solace in the knowledge that we should be back at the airport in several hours.

Soon after the two hotel guests were taken away, we overheard Torin arguing with someone else in the Xarantine language for a few minutes. Something was slammed onto a table. I almost left our room to investigate but decided instead to wait a few minutes.

We tried to sleep, but thinking about the unknown played havoc with our minds. Still, in this situation, I suggested to Sienna that discretion was the better part of valor. She followed my lead and took a deep breath. Thankfully, no more disturbances took place in those early morning hours.

The wake-up call rang at 9:30 a.m. and breakfast arrived at 10. We showered and got dressed, expecting the airport shuttle by 11 a.m. Sienna and I left our room and greeted Torin, who seemingly had not moved from his position hours before. Joe, Betty, and the four other travelers of our group joined us. None of them gave me any more information on the occurrence just hours before.

All eight of us were escorted down the elevator and the shuttle was already waiting outside the building. We took our seats as the driver inspected our passports and talked to the hotel attendant.

They spoke for about two minutes, at one point squabbling about something in Xarantine. We travelers looked at each other with some concern. The hotel employee then told the driver to wait as he ran back into the Best Eastern. Three long minutes later, he signaled the driver that we were okay to leave. Immediately, we let out a collective exhale.

En route to Xarantine International Airport, there was virtual silence as we looked at each other with wide eyes. We arrived at the sentry gate of the airport, and the armed guard briefly talked to our driver before opening the gate. We four couples were dropped off at the airport terminal and waved to our driver.

Once in the airport building, Joe approached Sienna and me and revealed a rumor he had heard from another transit hotel guest who was not in our group. They had briefly talked as both were standing just outside their adjacent rooms that morning.

Apparently, the two individuals apprehended at the Best Eastern Hotel were suspected of spying. They were traveling to Spain or France by way of Xarantine City and some plot was uncovered. It was unclear if the suspects were part of a larger organization.

Sienna was blown away, and I was caught by surprise. In this state of disbelief, we wandered around the airport until we eventually found the check-in counter of our airline. Our baggage was taken and boarding passes were assigned to us. In an hour, we boarded our flight for Dubai without any problems. Once in the air, Dubai in the United Arab Emirates was only a few hours away.

As I held my girlfriend's hand while we sipped some coffee, I asked the flight attendant if she knew of any unusual local news events that morning. She politely said no.

I then looked into the eyes of Sienna and we both mulled over the extraordinary events of the last ten hours. Almost simultaneously, we both became fully aware of how something as commonplace as a flight delay due to rain could indirectly lead to us being in proximity to a possible international espionage plot.

The hustle and bustle at an international airport

CHAPTER VI:
Multi-Sport

Certain people might be dismayed by the risk of trauma when participating in most any sport. But one accepts these possible dangers when he/she steps on the playing field. And I argue that this risk of physical injury is a requirement for any activity to be classified as sport.

In the course of my many past marathon races (see Chapter II), I have managed to stay free of major bodily injury. But I know of a good number of long-distance runners who were sidelined by conditions affecting the lower back and legs.

Here's an interesting question: At what point does a sport present more drawbacks than pluses, when the chance of injury outweighs the enjoyment factor? Friends tell me there is no universal answer.

I thought about the above query almost two years ago, trying to decide whether it was time to move on from the marathon to an alternative sport with less wear and tear on the body. Meanwhile, my fourth Palos Verdes Marathon and 14th overall was on the schedule for May of 2011. Right before my registration for the footrace, however, a close friend suggested a local duathlon instead.

"A du-what-lon?" I asked. "Do you mean a biathlon?"

My friend Mitch explained that a *duathlon* race combines the disciplines of running and cycling, but with three phases: first a run, then a transition to the bicycling segment of the competition, followed by another transition to the second running leg. The event is similar to the *traditional triathlon*, except the initial swimming portion is replaced by the run.

By contrast, a *biathlon*, be it a winter event or summer event, is comprised of two sports with two phases, one for each sport. To those familiar with the Olympics, there is only one true biathlon – the rigorous winter sport that involves the unusual combination of cross-country skiing and rifle shooting.

Astoundingly, there also exists the little-known competition of *modern biathlon* (or *biathle*). This world-class sport is comprised of a run then a swim then another run (essentially a duathlon with swimming instead of cycling in the middle portion of the race). Biathle world championships have actually been held every year since 1999.

Each of the aforementioned multi-sport events offers different challenges to the versatile athlete. All of these demanding disciplines also force the sportsman/sportswoman to decide how to allocate his/her training time for the different sports involved in the specific competition.

Continuing in his informative talk, Mitch explained to me the advantages of the duathlon over the marathon I was accustomed to. He said that compared to the marathoner, the duathlete is more well-rounded, with the cycling skill as the bridge between the two running segments. And by dividing his/her efforts between the two different activities, a duathlete lessens his/her risk of overuse injury.

The sport of bicycle racing is clearly tough on the lower body but much more forgiving on the bones and joints compared to running. Estimates have shown that your feet hit the ground with the force of two to four times your body weight during each stride of running. No such impact forces are involved in cycling.

With my interest piqued by the challenge of the multi-sport discipline of duathlon, I skipped the Palos Verdes Marathon and instead set my sights on the upcoming local duathlon, to be held in the coastal town of Encinitas, California. The event was only a month away, but I was already in reasonable shape to do well in the running segments. The cycling part was the novelty, as I had not been on a bike since my college years.

Not wishing to fork over hundreds or even thousands of dollars on a brand-new road bicycle, I asked my good friend Gary if he had a spare bike he could loan me for the race. Having participated and excelled in his share of triathlons, he owned several racing bicycles.

Graciously, he offered me a very nice red Cervélo road bike to borrow. I got on and realized the seat was probably too high. When Gary adjusted the seat, my rustiness on a bicycle was still apparent as I clumsily rode down the street.

Back in his garage, I then spied a smallish white bike in the corner. He pulled out the two-wheeler and described how it was collapsible and could fit in some car trunks. But it was probably the slowest bicycle he had.

He let me try out the portable cycle. Instantly, I felt comfortable in the seat and with the basic gear shifting capability on the handlebars. Maneuverability was surprisingly good as well.

I thanked Gary as he showed me how to collapse the bike, allowing it to fit in my car's trunk. No need for a car rack or hitch to transport the two-wheeler. He also loaned me one of his spare bicycle helmets, reminding me that this safety measure would be required in any race.

The next day, I went straight to a local road with a bike lane and began riding. My sense of balance seemed to have diminished after not cycling for all those years, but it soon returned. In no time, I was able to move faster and faster on the bike.

After I had ridden a few miles on the street, the shrill sound of a siren caught my attention as a police officer motioned me to stop. I asked the officer if I was moving too fast (not likely), but she shook her head.

"You should be wearing a helmet, sir. Have a safe ride."

In the state of California, bicycle helmets are required for cyclists under 18 years of age riding on public roads. But the helpful officer also reminded me that wearing a helmet could save my life. I bicycled back to my car and slapped on the protective headgear.

Over the next month, I ran only several miles a week but biked for many more hours. I got used to changing gears on the cycle and making turns and controlling my speed. Uphill routes were traversed with some difficulty. And some scratches and bruises were sustained when I fell off the bike on a few occasions during sharp turns.

During one of those falls, the bicycle chain became detached from the chain ring assembly. Fortunately, I had studied the parts of a road bike in the previous week and was able to reattach the chain by manipulating the *rear derailleur*.

On another incident, a flat tire was the result when I rode over some broken glass on the road. Fortuitously, a shopping mall with a sporting goods store was nearby. After I walked the bike to the shop, the bicycle technician adroitly changed the tire for a nominal fee.

At some point, learning such a skill may come in handy for me one day. But I reasoned that prevention of the problem in the first place should be more important. Were there ways to lessen the chance of a flat tire occurring at an inopportune time (such as during a race)? To answer this question, I talked to specialists in various bicycle shops to get their advice. In time, I became convinced that *tire liners* were the way to go.

These thin strips of synthetic material are positioned between the outer tire and the *inner tube* (the apparatus that holds the pressurized air in a tire). The tire liner serves to prevent small punctures of the tire from penetrating the inner tube, thus lessening the risk of a flat tire. One disadvantage, though, is that the tire liner adds several ounces of weight to your wheels, thus slowing you down to some degree.

After a few weeks of gaining some proficiency on the bike and improving my endurance, I felt ready for Encinitas and my first duathlon. I had clearly devoted many more hours of training to cycling compared to running on the road. But my legs did not ache at all.

As mentioned in Chapter II, somewhat worrisome in the preparations for past marathon races was my inability to get a good night's sleep before the competition. This situation was no different for my first duathlon, which had a start time of 7 a.m. With the combination of going to bed at an atypically early time and the pre-race excitement, grabbing some z's would again be difficult. I settled for catching 40 winks.

When my alarm clock went off on the morning of the race, it was still dark out. After awakening, I showered, ate, and put on my bike shorts and other sportswear. Gary's bike had been kept in the trunk of my car overnight, with helmet and sunglasses nearby. Upon leaving my house, I saw the sunrise and began my trip to Encinitas.

Few cars were on the freeway on that Sunday morning. Those with bikes hitched to their rears were likely being driven by fellow racers, I thought. Arriving at the race site, I encountered only some difficulty in finding a parking spot. A short while later, others joined me as we walked our bikes to the start line area.

My next priority was to find the *transition zone* (TZ), which is the epicenter of the multi-sport competition of duathlon. At this bustling area, dozens of large metal racks accommodate the bicycles of the many athletes. Near one's bicycle, each racer positions his/her various racing accessories (energy gels and drinks, sunglasses, helmet, towel, etc.).

The novice, such as myself in this duathlon, usually arrives relatively late and has to spend some valuable time finding a spot on the racks for his/her bike and sports gear. For the latecomer, this spot is usually located at an unfavorably far distance from the entry/exit gates of the TZ. Remember: The closer one is to the gates, the faster he/she can get to the bike and post a faster time in the race.

After finally finding a place to position my cycle on a rack, I checked the tire pressure and brakes. I applied some sunscreen and put on my sunglasses and cap. Next came the body markings.

To lessen the chance of theft of items stored in the TZ, each participant has his/her race number (and usually age) marked in black ink on an arm and on a leg. These same bib numbers are placed on one's bike, helmet, and racing shirt. As a competitor with these specific body markings, you have the privilege of entering and exiting the transition zone and roaming freely with the other athletes. Of course, you paid your registration fee to have this right.

How much to eat and drink before a race varies from athlete to athlete. For many, little food is ingested in the hour or two before race time while water and energy drinks are often imbibed before the competition begins. As a result, queues for the portable toilet facilities before the start of a race are understandably long.

Waiting in line, I chatted up a gal named Carla. Imagine Amy Adams with dark brown hair in a ponytail. She was quite upbeat despite noticing a flat tire on her bike just two hours before! It turned out that her neighbor was able to loan her a cycle on short notice for the race. In this Carla's third duathlon, I told my new acquaintance that I had the feeling she would make the most of her loaner bike.

Owing to the excitement and busyness and anticipation as race time approached, many athletes, unlike Carla, were not in the talking mood. They were clearly preoccupied with the various preparations needed that morning, from making sure race numbers were in place to confirming their bicycles' brakes were in working order. A good number of these competitors trained countless hours for this duathlon and were striving to maximize their performance on race day.

Some of the racers were competing for the first time while others were experienced athletes expecting to place in the top spots. Looking around before the start of the duathlon, I was impressed by the age range of participants, from teenagers to sexagenarians. Both men and women were well represented, but there was a higher proportion of male athletes.

In addition to the duathlon, a triathlon was to be run in the beach town of Encinitas that day, with both starting lines located in the same general area. A run along the beach was the first leg of the race for us duathletes, while triathletes would race toward the Pacific Ocean to begin their swim leg. Both triathletes and duathletes would converge during the bicycle and final running portions of their competitions.

All were now heading toward the starting line on the seashore as the transition zone was closed. A high level of collective energy was palpable in the cool morning air as athletes tensely waited for the contest to commence. We took off our hats as the national anthem was played. Cheering suffused the entire beach following the final lyrics of "… and the home of the brave."

One minute later, the gun sounded to mark the beginning of the duathlon, and I sped along the beach with the other racers. Sprinting on the sand at this early hour was no small task, and my legs felt the burn within half a mile. Many of the other competitors also began to slow down as they experienced the challenge of running on relatively dry sand. At that juncture, I wished that I had done more jogging in the previous weeks.

Toward the end of the arduous beach run, we struggled uphill on a paved path before reaching the TZ. Breathing hard, I eventually found my bike. Taking in a sports gel followed by water, I donned my helmet and quickly walked with the bicycle toward the exit area. The signal to mount the bicycle was given as I left the transition zone.

Riding a bicycle at a casual and relaxing speed is recreation. By contrast, pedaling a racing bike with force and determination during a duathlon is almost like a day at the office. Before long, I was dashing through the streets of Encinitas. The competition and adrenaline rush pushed me to cycle as fast as my body would allow, while fellow athletes were equally spirited.

As the bicycle leg of the duathlon continued, some real dangers soon became apparent. I was participating in a road race involving dozens of cyclists whizzing along on two-wheelers only a foot away from each other at times. Adding to this peril were those competitors who disregarded the rule of using the left lane only to pass another athlete. On one occasion, I felt the elbow of another duathlete on my *right* shoulder as he passed me on the course. It was a wonder that no collisions occurred, at least that I saw.

A few miles into the cycling portion of the contest, some of the triathletes had caught up to my group. They had completed their swim and were now sharing the bicycle course with us duathletes. More close calls occurred as additional racers moving at speeds in excess of 30 miles per hour entered an already crowded route.

I remember an incident when a cyclist on my left was attempting to pass me but instead was swerving toward me. Relying on my gut feeling, I decided to steer mildly to my right. In doing so, my bike came close to hitting the concrete curb of the sidewalk. Fortunately, I was able to successfully right my cycle away from the curb. The other competitor passed me, simply saying, "Sorry about that, bro!"

Toward the end of the bicycle leg was arguably the most exhilarating part of the duathlon – speeding through the steepest downhill of the race. Some people are afraid of high speeds on a bike, thinking that the frame may break or a tire may fall off. On a well-maintained cycle, those events are not likely to happen. But the threat of such disasters still remains.

Also, even with a bike in tip-top condition, there are clear risks when a cyclist is rapidly moving downhill. One can crash due to rocks or gravel or debris or a pothole, especially since it takes a much longer time to slow down or stop the bike going at high speeds. Wet areas on the road are not as easily avoided. And the bicycle is less maneuverable, making twisting roads more difficult.

On steep descents, I usually position my rear further back on the seat and use the front brakes almost exclusively, since most of the bike's weight is on the front wheel. And I will slow down more if the path is unfamiliar to me. Sharing the road with motorists further increases the risk of an accident when cycling downhill. Luckily, during my first duathlon, there were no motor vehicles on the bike route.

I experienced the thrill of going over 35 miles per hour on the downhill cycling portion of this competition, with no crashes or falls. Other athletes went even faster, appearing fearless in their need for speed.

The end of the bicycling part of the race was near, and I realized that my fingers were now tingling. This abnormal and uncomfortable feeling likely resulted from the frequent vibration of the speeding bicycle being transmitted to the nerves in my hands. Cycling gloves with padding would probably be part of my next race.

The transition zone was once again in sight, with race volunteers instructing us to dismount our bikes before entering the TZ on foot. Finding my specified area, I racked my bike and ingested another gel pack with water. The numbness in my hands would go away ten minutes later.

As I left the TZ for the last time in this race, the final running leg began as my racing cap replaced the helmet. Around me, other competitors displayed different levels of exhaustion. I also was witness to other forms of distress: A woman in her 20's vomited a small amount of water before continuing with her run, while a 30-ish man slowed down due to a leg cramp.

Training and conditioning determine a given athlete's performance once the final run phase is under way. By then, body stores of glycogen and glucose are being depleted while one's muscles are already being pushed to the limit. Many racers are content with just finishing at this point. Others push their bodies harder to achieve certain goals they set for themselves.

In this final stage of a race, water stations are crucial and usually plentiful. Otherwise, muscle cramps and overheating would become more common. I drank some water then poured some on my head at the last two water stations, attempting to avoid dehydration and heat exhaustion.

Perseverance was visible in the faces of all my fellow athletes as we ran the final miles. The blazing sun had emerged from behind the clouds, and we could hear distant cheers from spectators and volunteers and officials at the finish line. They were acknowledging the finishers one by one. These encouraging sounds strengthened our wills to plow on with our best efforts.

My feet were aching as the last 200 yards came into view. I noticed a mild side cramp in the area near my liver. And my muscles felt very sore due to lactic acid accumulation.

Despite the discomfort, I ran hard and crossed the finish line with a burst of speed. I then bent over with hands on knees while a volunteer draped a medal around my neck and strangers applauded my efforts. Some bottled water was offered to me, and it tasted like a sweet nectar because of my incredible thirst.

Around the post-race area, fruits and granola bars and muffins were available to all the finishers. Winners of some of the age groups were being announced. Nearby, a local band played "We Are the Champions" by Queen.

I felt a nudge on my upper back before seeing Carla at my side. She was all smiles with a medal of her own.

"That was quite the beach run," she exclaimed, recalling the start of the competition.

"I agree, but that last 200 yards was a bear!"

She went on to congratulate me on my first duathlon and commented, "My friend's bike was a little stiff, but I was happy to have it! Did your bike serve you well?"

"Other than some close calls, the bike felt good. By the way, kudos to you for defeating yours truly."

She went on to say that her finishing time was unexpectedly good for her. Even using her friend's bike.

No major injuries were sustained by either of us – definitely a cause for celebration. Once back at the transition zone, the two of us exchanged numbers then hugged each other goodbye. I struck up conversations with other competitors still around, all with different degrees of experience in the discipline of duathlon. All of the seasoned duathletes welcomed me to the sport.

I hung around for part of the medals ceremony, applauding the top finishers. In my mind, my cheers were also going out to the other participants who persevered to the end. Being a part of this sea of tired and sweaty and accomplished athletes, I became more convinced that this would not be my last duathlon.

The Solana Beach Duathlon

CHAPTER VII: Disabled List

Some things are beyond question – planetary motion, the global box office success of any James Bond film, and the craziness that is pickup basketball. The physicality, the unexpected foul calls, and the teamwork among relative strangers make this popular sport deliciously unpredictable. For these reasons, playing hoops has been a frequent recreational activity of mine since my high school years.

This demanding competition is available to almost everyone and requires no expensive equipment or lessons. And you can get a good idea about one's physical fitness and integrity by playing with or against him on the court for just an hour or two.

The game rewards those who are fast on their feet with good shooting and dribbling and passing skills. Having a durable body gives you an added advantage when it comes to the frequent physical contact and fouls. And relentless movement is required on the court, especially when playing dogged defense or boxing out others to capture a rebound.

Watching the professional game brings some statistics to mind. Boston Celtics 17 and Minneapolis/Los Angeles Lakers 16 in NBA championships. Kareem Abdul-Jabbar as the all-time scoring leader. Bill Russell having the most NBA titles. And the incomparable Michael Jordan with the highest scoring average in the regular season and NBA championship series.

In college, UCLA men have 11 national titles, with the University of Kentucky at 8. And who can forget Baylor University's Lady Bears, who on April 3rd of 2012 became the first collegiate basketball team ever (men or women) to win 40 games without a loss to capture the national championship.

Not headed to the NBA anytime soon, my fellow ballers and I have often gathered for half-court or full-court impromptu games. Most people joining us over the years have been competitive but not over-the-top. Rules of the game are casually discussed at the get-go, with infractions enforced by the group as a whole. Occasionally, a contest gets a little out of hand with more physical intensity than usual.

A few weeks after my first duathlon (see Chapter VI), I was involved in a pickup basketball game at an outdoor court on a Saturday afternoon. On that late spring day, play was rougher than usual, mostly because of a new 200-pound player named Jerome. He was a thickly built fire hydrant of a man. None of us knew this newcomer, but he seemed affable.

After an hour or more of playing a full-court game, all the players took a break and reached for their water bottles or sports drinks. Two ballers called it a day, and eight remained. We talked and agreed to set up new teams, four on four. Height was the main consideration as the new squads were established.

Everyone agreed on a half-court game, given the time of day and everyone's energy level. The contest began with high intensity on both sides but not as much as an hour before. After about 20 minutes, my team had built a lead of four baskets. The opposing squad, which included Jerome, then showed signs of frustration by committing more fouls. Rewarded with these fouls, my team made the most of its possessions with the ball.

As they fell further behind in the game, Jerome and his teammates were becoming even more physical in their defensive play. The stocky Jerome increasingly threw his weight around, and his fouls became more egregious. Some nasty words were expressed by several guys on both squads. I buttonholed my friend Skip on the opposing team and asked him to dial down the aggression of his fellow team members.

Still, everyone's enthusiasm did not cool down. During one of my team's possessions, I dribbled the ball into the key and attempted to drive past Jerome. He bumped me as I passed the free throw line, forcing me to backpedal a step. In an instant, I again moved into the lane, this time trying to get around Jerome's left side.

I managed to move past him for a moment before he grabbed my jersey. Using this grip, he swung my body around in a counterclockwise direction and to the ground, with my right forearm and elbow hitting the concrete first. At the same time, I instinctively grasped his jersey with my left hand and forced him to the hard ground. The back of his head hit the basketball court with a thump.

Play stopped as attention focused on Jerome and me. He was in a daze for a few seconds before getting up and saying, "I'm all right…nice drive."

It was clear, though, that Jerome's balance was impaired. We suggested he go to the hospital or at least stay a while so we could watch him. He thanked us but declined any help as he proceeded to leave the court.

Realizing that I was still on the ground, I felt a mild sting in my right elbow. There were bruises and cuts in my right forearm and elbow, but not much bleeding. One of the guys had a first aid kit in his car and applied some antiseptic and bandages on my arm. With already two injured players leaving the game, the others decided to stop play for that day.

After arriving home, I called Sienna to make plans for that Saturday night. Once I put the phone down, though, a surge of sharp pain appeared in my right elbow and forearm. An uncomfortable burning sensation accompanied the hurt. Taking off the bandages, I saw no active bleeding but there was redness and swelling and extreme hypersensitivity in the area from the elbow to the hand.

I explained the situation to my girlfriend, and she agreed to cancel our date and stop by in the morning. Meanwhile, I discovered that any movement involving my right arm (except for movements at the shoulder joint) caused extreme discomfort in the forearm and elbow areas. Writing only a few lines triggered significant pain. Even turning my arm the wrong way when I lay down or slept produced considerable hurt.

Consequently, other than writing with the right hand for short periods, I was forced to do almost everything with my left arm. Brushing my teeth, washing my face, taking a shower, holding the steering wheel. What were once simple tasks now proved to be monumentally complex. I felt almost as ineffectual as someone racing in the Iditarod with a team of Taco Bell chihuahuas pulling his sled (Thank comedian Dennis Miller's book *I Rant, Therefore I Am* for that image!).

The unremitting pain was barely tolerable, but I opted to avoid over-the-counter and prescription analgesic medicines so as not to mask the discomfort. Ice was applied at times to lessen the swelling and tenderness. Otherwise, my self-treatment to minimize the hurt involved using my right arm only when absolutely necessary.

Given the very limited right arm function, working at the office and writing notes would not be possible. I purchased a small notebook computer, and typing on it was tolerable. Still, the right elbow and forearm and wrist pains worsened with prolonged keyboard work.

I decided to see if a full schedule at work was possible. And it surprisingly was. The pain was intermittently severe, but I managed to get through each day. What was concerning to me, though, was the persistence of the significant discomfort after several days.

It was time to do an MRI scan of my right elbow. Six days after the injury, the results showed:

1. Radial head non-displaced fracture and associated osseous contusion.
2. Associated joint effusion, as well as edema within the supinator muscle adjacent to the radial head.

In English, I had fractured my right elbow and there was bruising and swelling in nearby structures in the forearm. There was now clear evidence of underlying structural damage in the arm.

A respected and experienced orthopedist colleague looked at the MRI films and examined my upper limb. He advised against surgery and gave me the option of wearing a brace (but no cast). Overall, his advice was reassuring to me, implying that healing should take place over time if further injury was avoided. I told him that I appreciated his recommendations and that I would put up with the painful problem sans brace for now.

The concept of long-standing discomfort after a trauma is humbling. Two people can experience the same accident and express vastly different pain complaints. A plethora of factors is in play, including personality, general physical fitness, antecedent pain threshold, and cultural beliefs. For example, it has been shown that an extrovert who is generally confident and active will be less likely than a wallflower to develop a chronic pain condition.

Of course, more severe tissue damage, especially to nerve fibers, forbodes a more prolonged recovery time as well.

In my neurology practice, I treat various types of pains due to different types of injuries and illnesses. Treatment options include physical therapy, various medicines, injections, surgery, and alternative medicine and therapies if clearly indicated. The possible ways to manage the discomfort are relayed to my patients and they decide on the plan for managing their pains.

Now, I was the patient.

Continuing to eschew medicines, I opted instead to endure the hurt and tenderness without complaint. I limited right arm activity as much as possible, kept my wounds clean, and used ice on occasion. To promote the healing process, I also maintained a regular sleep schedule and ingested sufficient protein in my diet.

As my painful ordeal dragged on, I surprisingly felt invigorated to some degree each day, probably due to elevated adrenaline and cortisol levels related to the distress. The continuous discomfort both tormented and energized me at the same time!

After a few weeks, I became more and more aware that no one knew exactly how long the pain would last. It would have been just as easy for me to become frustrated and depressed because of the unrelenting aches in my arm. But I chose to remain optimistic and hopeful and essentially roll with the punches. In essence, I tried to become comfortable with the discomfort.

My patience was eventually rewarded.

Four weeks after the sports injury, my right arm pains started to slowly diminish. No infection appeared as I changed bandages regularly. I gradually was able to use my hand and forearm more and more in basic tasks, but forceful movements were not yet possible.

Fortunately, I did not fall victim to a chronic pain syndrome, which can develop in any given person after an injury like mine. In such a syndrome, the pain due to traumatic injury (or non-traumatic illnesses) becomes constant and persistent. There is no spontaneous improvement over time, and this medical condition can continue for months or years and become disabling.

I did not resume playing basketball until about two months after my injury. But when I did make that first dribble and shoot that first ball toward the hoop, I felt a sense of both relief and triumph.

About a fortnight later, I saw Jerome shooting some hoops on his own at the gym's basketball court. He was wearing a soft neck brace. It was crystal clear that he was moving slowly and that his head and neck motions were limited.

As I approached him, he said, "Hey, I remember you. How's the arm?"

We exchanged injury stories and some jokes. Jerome's brace would be coming off in a few weeks, and it turned out he suffered a hairline fracture in a spine bone of the lower neck. No operation was required, but he was not allowed to participate in any rigorous contact sports for at least another month.

Soon after his neck brace came off, Jerome returned to the court and greeted me and some friends. We set up the teams, and I was again playing head-to-head against Jerome in a full-court pickup basketball game. We battled with an intensity that showed our will to win. But from that time on, we would never again be involved in any knockdown type of fouls against each other.

To a considerable extent, Lady Luck had smiled upon us as we were both able to overcome our injuries without any major sequelae. And by coping with adversity, my fellow basketballer and I probably learned a lot about ourselves as we went through our difficult experiences.

Just as importantly, I have realized how an injury can change your life. If you are fortunate, the change is just a temporary placement on the disabled list of weekend warriors.

In the end, we athletes all accept the inherent dangers while playing sports. And we probably do so because risk-taking can lead to strong feelings of self-determination and satisfaction. But each person has to answer the question of how much risk is acceptable. As for me, I rely on one of the central maxims carved into the Temple of Apollo in Delphi, Greece:

Know thyself.

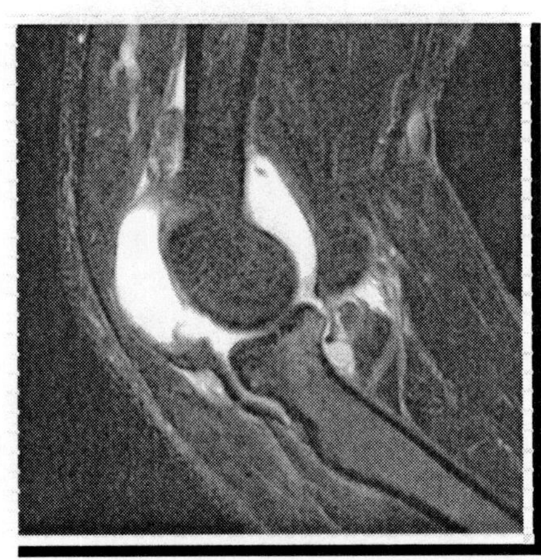

Radial head fracture on MRI

CHAPTER VIII:
Triathlon

For the person who is usually very active, being immobilized because of some injury or any type of illness can be quite dispiriting. Still, it is best to limit strenuous activity during the recovery phase so that nutrients and the body's energy stores can be focused on the healing process.

After being a virtual homebody for over a month after my right arm injury (see Chapter VII), I began to notice that function and strength were slowly improving in the affected limb. As I had mentioned, I returned to the basketball court as soon as was possible, just happy to be shooting and dribbling and passing the ball again with both hands.

The fracture and contusions in my right arm, occurring less than a month after my first race, also interrupted my progress in the duathlon pursuit (see Chapter VI). However, approximately six weeks after the injury, I felt ready to tackle my second duathlon. That would take place near the famous strawberry fields in Oxnard, northwest of Los Angeles, California.

Eerily, the competition would be held during the weekend known as "Carmageddon I" in the City of Angels ("Carmageddon II" would take place over a year later). From Friday night until Sunday night, a five-mile stretch of the very busy Interstate 5 was closed to all traffic due to renovations. As a result, a minor panic appeared in those planning to use the extensive freeway system that weekend.

On the day of the duathlon, my main concern was losing grip of the bike's handlebars with my recovering right hand. Some pain in my right arm was present during the race, even during the running phases, but it was relatively minor. I was able to steer the cycle without difficulty, and my finish time for the race was respectable given the circumstances. On the way home, contrary to predictions for that weekend, there were no major delays in the Los Angeles freeway system.

In the ensuing weeks, I continued to feel energetic and took part in two more duathlons, this time in San Diego County. For both of these contests, my race times improved in the running as well as cycling segments. At the Imperial

Beach Duathlon, I also ran into a former female patient in the transition zone after the race.

At Imperial Beach, a triathlon was run together with my duathlon event. Recall that in Chapter VI, I stated that the only real difference between a duathlon and a traditional triathlon is that the initial running leg of the former is replaced with a swim leg for the latter. Accordingly, many triathlon events are held together with duathlon competitions.

After some thought, I realized that in essence, a duathlon is preferred by those who enjoy the thrill of multi-sport races but are unable to swim to save their lives. At that point, I was the quintessential duathlete.

Still, the sport of triathlon was very appealing to me as a true test of one's sports versatility. It remained to be seen whether I could become skilled enough in the water to become a triathlete.

I did not grow up spending much time at the lake or in the ocean. It follows that the high school pool was my introduction to the sport of swimming. At physical education class, the instructor told us to jump into the water and show him what we could do. My ability to glide and propel myself through the water was satisfactory when I was underwater and holding my breath. The problem was getting air into and out of my lungs consistently.

Many students were in my PE class, so the teacher focused his efforts on those less able than myself. I enjoyed swimming well enough, but my inability to get a good breath and swim for any meaningful distance diminished my interest in any water sports outside PE class.

Soon after my fourth duathlon competition, I made a commitment to expand my athletic range and enter my first triathlon. This challenge forced me to become proficient in my Achilles' heel at the time – endurance swimming. Furthermore, there was another incentive for me to improve my swimming: This sport is one of the best total body workouts, incorporating most of the body's 650+ muscles, with little stress on the joints.

Owing to the wonders of the Internet, videos on how to swim well were abundant. Soon, I gained the insight that many poor swimmers overlook – one exhales primarily underwater and inhales when the head is above water. Prior to this revelation of sorts, I had attempted to exhale and inhale in rapid succession in the brief time my head was above water, a very difficult and exhausting technique.

Fortunately, my gym membership for years has included access to several local facilities, including those with indoor pools. Finding the closest gym with a pool, I applied the exhale-in-water and inhale-out-of-water principles. At first, I inhaled my share of irritating chlorinated water. With diligent practice, though, I made steady progress. Before I knew it, swimming without breathlessness for 25 to 50 yards at a time became possible. At that juncture, the next step was bettering my swimming stroke.

Any swim stroke can be used in a triathlon, but the crawl or freestyle is the most popular, due to its speed and relatively low energy requirement for distance traveled. The online how-to videos were again helpful. I eventually applied the many pointers they gave me: tightly cupping one's hands to grab water in the pull phase of the stroke, rotating the body along its axis to move through the water with minimal resistance, breathing on alternate sides on every third stroke to promote symmetric muscle development, and so on.

As I practiced in the water using the above principles, important strides were being made toward my first triathlon. Even so, I was aware that professional help would be invaluable. Taking some swimming lessons at the local YMCA allowed me to improve my mechanics and form. I learned to swim more horizontally, reach out with my arm more before the pull phase of the stroke, and use the hourglass-shaped pull method with the arms.

At the class, I made some new friends, none of whom would be entering a triathlon any time soon. Jade, a lithe 32-year-old from Argentina, wanted to be able to keep up with her boyfriend, a swimmer since high school. Also taking the class was Tim, who had the frame of a sprinter and would be trying out for his school water polo team in a few months. And there was Nina, a Texas native with freckles, who just never got around to learning how to swim when she was younger. Once the lessons ended and we said our farewells, it dawned on me that my first triathlon was only a few weeks away.

When the sport of triathlon first appeared is up to debate. Some enthusiasts claim it began in a Paris suburb in the 1920's as an event called Les Trois Sports (The Three Sports). Many agree that the first modern triathlon took place in San Diego, California, in the 1970's, following the format of the current *reverse triathlon* (running then cycling then swimming). Forty-six finishers (including 11 women) made history on that weekday evening of September 25th 1974.

For those who have seen a present-day *traditional triathlon* (with the usual order of swimming than cycling then running), the opening 200 yards or so of swimming are tumultuous. The early morning combination of thrashing arms and shoulders, legs seeming to kick in all directions, and the individual struggles to get a good breath every few strokes is an experience best avoided for most athletes.

As the swim leg progresses, the same series of aforesaid events takes place in the crowded spaces around the turning buoys and can be equally unnerving. Add to the mix the cold temperatures, rough water, and poor visibility in an open water swim and one wonders why people actually *pay* to participate in such sporting events.

I am surprised that many triathletes are not aware of the *reverse triathlon* format, which uses the running then cycling then swimming sequence. Just the other day, I was in a running shoes specialty store and talking with a man who had completed five triathlons. He had not even heard of a reverse triathlon. My good friend Gary, who has raced in several triathlons at various distances, was also unaware of the reverse triathlon concept until I enlightened him.

For the aspiring triathlete, the framework of the reverse triathlon makes a lot of practical sense. Swimming in aquatic complexes in the reverse triathlon does not require quality full-body wetsuits, which are essential in cold water ocean swimming in the traditional triathlon and can cost you hundreds of dollars. It is easier to warm up your body during the initial running leg with the reverse format than during the chilly early morning swim portion of the traditional triathlon. And for those like me with a durable upper body, performing the swimming leg last is not too strenuous.

It was a cool September morning in Apple Valley, California. This town of 70,000, northeast of Los Angeles and about a 90-minute drive from the Rose Bowl Stadium, lies on the southern edge of the Mojave Desert. My girlfriend Sienna and I had driven to this 3000-foot-high municipality the night before and stayed at a hotel only a few miles from the race site. My cell phone alarm woke us at 4 a.m., but Sienna stayed in bed while I made preparations.

After showering and eating, I rolled the bike out of the hotel room to the car and secured it on the car rack. My running cap, bicycle helmet, sunglasses, racing gloves, swim goggles, towel, and sunblock were packed into the gym bag. I nudged Sienna, who then got up, showered, put on a sweatshirt and shorts, and grabbed an apple and bagel to eat on the way.

We drove to the town hall area for the Apple Valley Fall Festival, which included a 5K run and 10K run along with the reverse triathlon. Arriving an hour and a half before race time, I was free to choose my spot in the transition zone (TZ) to rack up my bike and position my race materials.

As usual, I did not get much quality sleep the previous night, with the unusually early bedtime and excitement about my first triathlon. By contrast, Frank, an Eli Manning look-alike I met at the TZ, informed me he had slept well the night before by just thinking and dreaming about past experiences running country trails. I'll try that for my next race, I told him.

The volunteers at the registration tent were perky for the morning hour. I obtained my bib numbers and timing chip. After securing the numbers on the bike, helmet, and racing shirt, I still had 30 minutes to kill before race time. During that half hour, I unexpectedly ran into Karl, a former policeman whom I had met at the Imperial Beach Duathlon the month before. At that contest, mention was made of my plans to do the Apple Valley Triathlon. He apparently was intrigued by the idea and later decided to sign up himself for his first triathlon.

At 7 a.m. sharp, the main event announcer welcomed all competitors on the nippy Saturday morning. He presented a local celebrity, who gracefully sang the Star Spangled Banner. Sienna, still sleepy, embraced me and wished me good luck. She would take a short nap in the car before later going to the finish line at the aquatic complex.

All the racers seemed relaxed, and we gathered around the starting line. Suddenly, a bell was rung, indicating that the reverse triathlon was under way. At the outset, we ran on a mildly bumpy dirt trail. The scenic mountains and crisp air energized me as I began the journey in my first triathlon.

In this first part of the race, though, my conditioning was clearly subpar since I had chosen to spend more time in the pool than on the road in the last month. Even though I had conquered marathons in the past, the lack of regular running in recent weeks resulted in a drop in my endurance. My pace was noticeably slower than usual as the running route moved into local streets.

Fortunately, this initial running portion was on flat ground with no hills in sight. I stopped at the water stations to take short breaks and replenish lost fluids. As I left one of the water stops, another athlete, a 40-year-old local wearing a bright orange cap, ran up beside me.

"Just hate this first part," he said, "with all the banging on our legs. Don't you? Can't wait to get to the cycling part."

I could not have agreed with him more, being a man allergic to running until just a few years prior.

The entire pack of almost 200 competitors was moving at a fairly rapid pace, with a group of ten runners leading the field. As each mile passed, the distance increased between participants. No one stopped due to cramps or injury, though, meaning that all the training had paid off. At the last water station in the running leg of the race, I took in a sports gel along with a cup of water.

We all neared the end of the run and entered the TZ. Most athletes appeared relatively fresh. Meanwhile, I had warmed up midway into the run and my leg soreness early in the race was now gone. Taking off my running cap, I quickly fastened the straps of the bike helmet as I guided the cycle out of the transition zone.

After getting on the bike, I sped past a fellow athlete to begin the bicycling portion of the triathlon. This second phase of the race would involve 15 miles through local streets and roads. There were some challenging uphill climbs, and we shared the road with motorists on parts of the path. On some of the downhill sections, my bike speedometer registered velocities above 35 miles per hour.

On one of the hills, I saw a racer walking her bike the other direction. She had incurred a flat tire and was unable to repair the leak. A little further up the hill, a clean-cut stocky man in his 30's was pushing his cycle, needing the break due to prostration.

No accidents took place as we cyclists sometimes rapidly moved past each other only a few feet away. The cool wind on our faces helped neutralize the warm sun that morning. On a flat stretch of the race, I spotted some roadkill, a squirrel I think. One racer almost skidded trying to get around the animal remains.

The 15-mile ride was stimulating but also exhausting. Some athletes did not finish the race because of the uphill sections. At the other extreme, the faster participants in this phase had a significant advantage in the overall competition, since the bike portion is always the longest leg of any triathlon.

With my legs feeling a little tight, I finally rode toward the transition zone before dismounting as instructed. Racking my bike, I ingested another sports gel packet with water. All clothes and accessories came off except for my swim trunks, and I snatched my goggles and ran barefoot on the pebbly path to the aquatic center. Once at the large outdoor pool, the prospect of six laps faced me before my goal of becoming a triathlete would be realized.

Swimming the first two lengths, I focused on maintaining good form and breathing on alternate sides in the crawl stroke. It was fairly congested in each lane as the many competitors sought to pass one another. By the second length, I tried to pick up the pace as much as possible despite my dwindling energy stores. Slowing down near the wall of the pool, I then swam under the divider to prepare for the third lap in the next lane.

About 15 yards into this lap, I felt a jolt near my left ear, followed by a brief feeling of vibration throughout my head. Another swimmer's right elbow had struck me accidentally as he tried to pass me. Other racers were closely in pursuit so he and I swam on.

At the end of the lane, I stopped for a few seconds to catch my breath as he yelled, "Sorry about the elbow. My bad!"

I accepted his apology and moved on to lane four, trying to make up some time and get past other swimmers. In my heightened adrenaline state, my leading arm hit the right foot of a tattooed head-shaven man in front of me. He was forced to stop and hold on to the lane divider in the pool. With other racers behind me, I decided to continue down the lane.

As I moved under the lane divider near the wall to start the fifth lap, I took a gander at my tattooed fellow competitor, who was still holding on to the floating plastic divider. Evidently, his foot sustained more of a blow than I had expected.

It was now the fifth swimming lap, and my arms and legs were tiring to some degree. A sharp pain was felt and a brief buzzing sound was heard in my left ear. But my aim was to finish well and give it my all. I could hear the crowd cheering finishers in the next lane.

After making my last turn at the swimming pool wall, I continued my freestyle stroke into the final lap. Just ahead of me, a yellow-capped swimmer slowed down to catch her breath and briefly stopped to take hold of the pool edge. I would pass her, and I later saw her resuming her last lap using the less strenuous and also slower breaststroke. Her diligence in completing the triathlon at all costs was admirable.

In the last 15 yards of the sixth and final lap, my body felt like it weighed 300 pounds. With the finish in sight, I fought on and made steady progress toward the end of the lane as I struggled to maintain good form in the water. The local crowd and those triathletes who had already completed their race roared as I exited the pool and crossed the finish line. A cheery volunteer draped a finisher's medal around my neck and put her arm around my shoulder.

I joined some other happy athletes in the recovery area, and we cheered on the remaining racers. After several minutes, Kris, the head-shaven man I had accidently hit in the fourth lap, emerged from the pool and finished the race. He ended up swimming the last two laps with the sidestroke since he still felt the effects of my blow to his right foot.

"Does it still hurt?" I asked, approaching Kris as he turned in his timing chip.

After being told that I was the one who hit his leg, he said, "So you're the freaking guy! I ought to…"

He swung his right arm back, then a grin appeared on his face.

"Just kidding, man. I'm sure you didn't mean to. Did you?"

"Nah," I laughed. "But I compliment you on dealing with the foot, improvising, and finishing the race with the sidestroke."

I had finally done it! By completing this reverse triathlon at the Apple Valley Fall Festival, I joined the triathlon nation. Sienna found me and planted a congratulatory kiss on my cheek. She asked me if it was all worth it, and I nodded resoundingly.

"Other than some sore feet, a little sunburn on my face, and a small bump near my left ear, no harm done," I said candidly.

Walking back to the transition zone, Sienna and I ran into Frank, the triathlete I met in the TZ before the race. He had run this race the last four years, and he placed third in his age group that day.

"Very impressive," I remarked, shaking his hand vigorously.

We got to talking about how he got started in the sport, and Frank admitted that he has stayed with the reverse triathlon format for most all of his races, having done a traditional triathlon only once.

"It just makes more sense to swim last," he asserted.

To me, he was preaching to the choir.

Jill, Frank's girlfriend, showed up and the four of us enjoyed the hospitality of the event organizers, with various fruits and muffins and even hot dogs offered near the aquatic complex. A deejay played music using a surprisingly huge sound system. As stated earlier, the triathlon was but one part of this Apple Valley celebration, and many families were on hand for this event either at poolside or in the adjacent park enjoying a picnic.

To date, I have completed ten triathlons in the reverse format. As noted earlier, the first modern triathlon in San Diego in 1974 was also a reverse triathlon. In the United States, the largest reverse triathlon has taken place in Hemet, California, for 27 years now. This Tinsel Triathlon is held each December, with almost a thousand participants running and cycling and swimming each year. En route to the event last year, my car's external thermometer indicated a brisk 30 degrees Fahrenheit.

For those who desire the ultimate experience, the Ironman triathlon is a lengthy 2.4-mile swim *combined with* 112 miles of cycling *followed by* a full 26.2-mile marathon! You can appreciate this vainglorious quote by then U.S. Navy commander John Collins, who developed the Ironman concept in 1978:

"Swim 2.4 miles! Bike 112 miles! Run 26.2 miles! Brag for the rest of your life!"

It is no stretch to say that I may join the ranks of the traditional triathletes in the near future. I will leave the Ironman to the professionals, though.

So what does motivate someone to do his/her first or 10th or 50th triathlon? Reasons can include relieving stress, social interactions in triathlon clubs, boosting of one's self-confidence, and weight loss. Others compete for bragging rights or the chance to wear cool sportswear and ride flashy bikes.

As for me, I like to think of the competition and overall fitness benefits. Setting goals, meeting like-minded athletes, interacting with nature and the weather. The satisfaction of facing the hardships of training and beating the next guy/gal, but still avoiding injury. And, despite the title of the fifth James Bond film, you actually only live *once*!

The Pasadena Triathlon

CHAPTER IX: Land of the North

Have you been searching for a hidden gem that offers a plethora of novel outdoor adventures? Where whale-watching is one of the most popular tourist activities and the number one attraction is the soothing geothermal spa at the Blue Lagoon? If so, the small island nation of Iceland awaits you.

This wonderful Scandinavian country of over 300,000 is among the least densely populated on Earth, and two-thirds of Icelanders live in the pretty city of Reykjavík, which has the distinction of being the world's northernmost capital.

Arriving at Keflavík International Airport on a nippy October morning, Sienna and I deboarded the airplane and walked toward the airport terminal. We inhaled fresh cool air as our fellow passengers followed us across the tarmac. By chance, everyone was astounded to see a large passenger jet nearby marked with the words

"Iron Maiden: The Final Frontier World Tour 2011." Would this classic English heavy metal band be performing during our stay?

Feeling our body temperatures rise as we walked through the automatic doors into the terminal building, my girlfriend and I followed the signs saying *KomufarÞegar* and *Vegabréfaeftirlit* (Icelandic for Arrivals and Passport Control). After a short wait in line, we moved forward and were greeted by the orderly and friendly airport personnel, who stamped our passports and directed us to the car rental area.

The rules of driving in Iceland are straightforward: Drive on the right, fasten your seat belts, and refrain from handheld cell phone use. In addition, you should keep your headlights on, slow down when the road changes from paved to gravel, and keep the number 112 handy in case you need the Icelandic National Police.

I started up the Kia Sportage 4x4 SUV and Sienna and I exited the airport grounds. We could not help but noticing the large metallic sculpture in a pond just outside the airport terminal, looking like a little hook attached to a giant steel egg. Actually, the artwork is named the *Jet Nest*, representing a jet wing or airplane "hatching out of its egg," as described by an airport official.

On the nicely-paved highway to the capital 30 miles away, we gazed at clear skies, various blue signs in Icelandic, some mountains in the distance, and dark rock formations. The ride was relaxing, with few cars in sight. Sienna and I decided to stop in the small town of Vogar for some snacks.

When we arrived in Reykjavík, our first stop was the Perlan building, which houses the Saga Museum of Icelandic history. This architecturally-elegant structure offered a deck with panoramic 360-degree views, as well as a fine rotating restaurant completing a full revolution in two hours. The exterior, though, was the main attraction: a glass dome set on six huge water storage tanks on top of the Oskjuhlid Hill overlooking the city.

Following dinner, we eventually found our quaint hotel. After a long day of travel, Sienna and I slept soundly in our modest but charming room. The next morning, we took in some Icelandic pancakes before exploring more of the coastal capital city.

Strolling around town, we visited landmarks like the imposing Hallgrímskirkja church, the nearby statue of Viking explorer Leif Eriksson, the Austurvöllur downtown square, and the small but scenic Lake Tjörnin. In the evening, we got a taste of the Reykjavík nightlife, dancing to the local music beat and sipping *brennivín* (which literally means "burning wine").

Rays of light between the curtains of our hotel room landed on our faces the next morning.

Sienna awoke just before me and pushed me gently on the shoulder. She showed me that look that reflected a certain *je ne sais quoi* that always appealed to me.

"Are we really going to do this?" asked Sienna while stretching in bed.

"I think we went a long way to back out now," I replied.

After a breakfast that included *hafragrautur* (a type of oatmeal that is a staple in Iceland) and some *skyr* (yogurt), my adventurous girlfriend and I fastened our seat belts and drove out of our hotel to a site about two hours southeast down the coast. We brought with us warm jackets and gloves for the gest planned for that day.

Looking at our trusty map, we turned off the main road and drove for another half hour on a gravelly path. Soon, Sienna and I arrived at our destination – the foot of the Sólheimajökull glacier in South Iceland. It was cloudy that morning, typical for the time of year, even though the name Sólheimajökull translates to "Home of the Sun Glacier."

A glacier is a large ice formation, and the vast majority of these massive but shrinking structures lie in gigantic ice sheets in the areas of the North and South Poles. Sólheimajökull itself is part of the Mýrdalsjökull ice cap (one of the big four in Iceland). As most of you know, glaciers are frequently melting, evolving, and moving. With these basic facts in mind, I found it prudent that my girlfriend and I explore our first glacier with expert guidance.

Within minutes, we found the rugged Dagur (which means "day" in Icelandic) and his four other pupils for that day. A restrained enthusiasm was evident in us novices, while Dagur was all smiles, expressing a quiet confidence. All of us introduced ourselves to the Icelander, much like game show contestants saying a little about themselves to the host. Not one had done anything like this before, and each and every one of us was a first-time visitor to the Land of the North.

Our guide proceeded to lead us to the equipment we would need for the upcoming activities. He first instructed us on the use of the *crampons*, a necessity when hiking on any icy surface. These metal devices were fastened to our boots with a binding system, much like how skis attach to ski boots. The spikes on the crampons gripped the ice and allowed us to walk on the glacier surface with a sense of security. As expected, it took a little while for us to get used to walking with these gadgets on.

We were each given an *ice axe*, a tool we would find invaluable. It could be used as a walking stick, an anchor to stop a fall or slide, a device to cut into the snow for creating "steps" or "stairs," and as a gizmo for other functions. Some of us joked around and began to joust with our axes before Dagur told us the dangers of doing so.

Further instructions and safety tips on the correct use of our crampons and ice axes were provided by our capable Icelandic guide. Helmets and ropes were then distributed to all. With backpacks in place, our group followed in single file behind Dagur. This manner of walking was important to ensure that where we were stepping was safe.

As we set off on our hike that morning, it was very apparent that we were moving rather slowly. This casual pace was predictable since all of us novices were galumphing, carefully pushing our crampon spikes into what was essentially a massive piece of solid, uneven, and slippery ice. As the six of us slowly adapted to using the crampons, we stopped often to admire this fascinating glacial world and listen to our professional attendant.

Dagur, who looked like Jason Statham but with more hair, was impressive. In our trek, he was quite the cognoscente, able to answer any and all questions that came his way. Our leader described how a glacier forms and moves, how the various ice formations developed over time, and why glaciers are so important to the world. He even interspersed his informative talks with some lighthearted jokes that were actually quite humorous.

There was a definite uphill slope in our glacial hike that challenged the fitness of some in the group. But the effort was very worthwhile. We appreciated the otherworldly scenery of a land that few see. Ice tunnels, blue ice in different hues, dangerous crevasses and moulins, seracs, snow bridges, and other spectacular terrain. To make it more memorable, there was even some sprinkling of hail off and on.

About two hours into the excursion, a shrill scream from behind me caught everyone's attention. Sienna and I turned and saw Daphne, a slim brunette from Lyon, France, on the ice. She pointed at her left ankle and was in obvious pain.

She consented as I removed her hiking boot and sock and examined her left foot and ankle. There was tenderness at the ankle but no swelling, and range of motion was good. I suspected a mild or first degree sprain, or overstretched ligament. Recalling that I had packed some aspirin in case of emergency, I opened my backpack and gave two tablets to Daphne.

As she lay on the snow, our injured traveler reported that her pain was slowly improving. While she was recovering, Dagur tried to distract the group with some history of his native Iceland and its original settlement in the late 9th century by Norsemen. He reminded us that Iceland has a population of only 300,000 (half of that of Vermont) and joined NATO in 1949. Also, there is no standing army in this nation.

Maybe 40 minutes after her initial cry, Daphne was back on her feet with only mild discomfort. I checked on her ankle and foot and noted that the tenderness had decreased. She was told that it was okay to put on her sock and boot with crampon. Soon, she was able to bear weight on her legs and walk with ease. We all agreed that this arctic adventure would continue.

Our guide eventually led us to a small valley almost surrounded by massive walls of ice. He then queried the group: "Is anyone up for ice climbing?"

Sienna and I had done some indoor wall climbing in the past but never ice climbing. After Daphne of all people and her companion raised their hands, I did the same and pushed up Sienna's as well. My girlfriend was mildly perturbed by my presumption but encouraged by my confidence in her.

For you indoor wall climbers out there, let me give you my honest opinion: Ice climbing by far is more rigorous. First of all, there are the cold temperatures and the challenge to stay warm. Secondly, there is the need to use an ice axe in each hand to propel oneself up the wall. Finally, there is much effort required to grab or grip the ice with the crampons attached to your boots.

Before any ice climbing was to occur, however, I wanted to assure optimal safety first. Of course, this was also Dagur's priority – dead or injured customers are bad for business.

This assurance was possible for us beginners because of a sturdy roping system that was fastened to any given ice climber. The rope goes through metallic loops (*carabiners*) which are tightly fastened to the ice by way of anchors at critical points above the level of the climber. The expert Dagur would serve as the *belayer* on the ground, able to pull on the rope as needed and prevent the ice climber from having a major fall.

The initial four in our group who had expressed the intent to ascend the ice wall soon became three as Daphne reconsidered. The remaining trio played rock-paper-scissors to decide the first one to give it a go. I was victorious and walked to Dagur to get connected to the roping system. An ice axe was then placed in each of my hands.

As the end of the safety line or rope was fastened around my waist, I followed Dagur's orders and swung the ice axe in my left hand high to the ice, allowing the tool to embed into the ice wall. Soon after, my right arm forcefully drove the other axe into the wall above. With the axes planted on the frozen water, I then kicked my left boot into the ice with enough force to allow the crampon to stick. Subsequently, I rapidly moved my right foot into the wall and the sharp crampon gripped the ice once again. In the process, an ice climber was born.

From that point on the wall, I slowly climbed up the ice. I pulled one axe off the ice wall and extended that arm to drive the tool to a higher level. I did the same with the other ice axe. Afterwards, one boot with crampon would be released and then driven to a higher position on the ice, followed by a similar movement with the opposite leg. Once at the new elevation, I would push my body forward to touch the wall, stabilize my body, and prepare for the next cycle.

Alternatively, I learned that I could release one boot from the ice and embed it to a higher level, do the same with the other boot with crampon, then swing one then the other ice axe to a higher point on the ice wall.

In time, I began to use different combinations of moving any one of my limbs (with crampon or ice axe) at any given time to allow me to scale up the wall. The most important task was to securely grip the ice with the crampons and ice axes before releasing any of them from the ice wall to move to a higher level.

After performing only about a dozen of the aforesaid maneuvers, I realized the full-body workout I was getting. On top of that, I had to remain alert since a wrong move could cause me to slip off the wall. Fortunately, such a fall was not likely to be significant with the safety line around me connected to the attentive Dagur on the ground below.

Slowly but surely, I made progress up the semi-steep ice wall, becoming more confident in my technique using axes and crampons to defy gravity. Looking below, I saw the images of Dagur, Sienna, and the other spectators become smaller as their voices became softer.

Once at the top of the formidable 40-foot wall of ice, I beheld the incredible vista of Sólheimajökull and the surrounding mountains. It was quite an electrifying moment. I let out a loud "Yes! Yes! Yes!" to the group below. Some generous cheers and whistles followed.

A few minutes later, Sienna, winning the coin flip to go next, began her climb up the wall with Dagur as her safety net. Having witnessed my inaugural experience in this challenging sport, she felt confident she could do the same.

Once she became accustomed to the general technique of planting an ice axe or crampon into the ice, followed by the release of a different axe or crampon from the wall, then repeating the process, Sienna was moving up the ice wall in no time. About three quarters of the way up, though, her arms began to tire from her swinging of the axes. Dagur safely led her down to terra firma.

Georges, Daphne's friend who could pass for a young Jean-Claude Van Damme, would be the last climber of the day. He took more chances than me and ascended at a more rapid pace. As he continued with this approach, his crampons slipped off the ice several times, but the alert Dagur prevented any falls as he belayed Georges with the safety ropes. In the end, the Frenchman also successfully reached the top of the ice wall and showed me a good fist pump.

The exhilarating experience made all of us forget about the cold temperatures and gusts of wind. Some hail showered on us. By this time, our gloved fingers were becoming mildly numb. After some discussion, the group agreed to head back.

On the return voyage, the six of us followed Dagur in a less organized fashion. We were able to walk faster as we had gotten used to moving with the crampons, but the precipitation forced us to slow down. The hail was becoming heavier as the skies remained gray.

Throughout the day's trek, everyone could not help but notice the ubiquitous black substance covering much of the glacier. Dagur informed us that the finer ash particles had come from a nearby volcanic eruption a few years ago, while the coarser black material originated from an event almost a hundred years ago. Once again, our leader seemed to be omniscient.

As we traversed the field of ice, we also heard the sporadic sounds of rapidly flowing water. Thanks to Dagur, we learned that rushing streams underneath the ice surface were everywhere. And they were reminders of how the ice and water in this glacier were always in a state of flux.

Before long, the tip of Sólheimajökull was in sight. Sienna and I took a final long look around us as the last crevasse was safely crossed by the group. By then, except for Dagur, the entire bunch was tired and feeling the effects of the cold.

We all expressed our gratitude to our able guide before removing our crampons. Our ice axes and ropes and helmets were returned in a semi-organized fashion. After exchanging emails and saying farewells, the group dispersed and thought about the amazing day we had just experienced.

Sienna gazed into my eyes and said "Wow!"

I felt the same way.

After glimpsing the scenic glacier and surrounding terrain one last time, my girlfriend and I searched for and eventually found our Kia SUV rental under overcast skies. She drove us carefully out of the unpaved area before reaching the main road. Leisurely, we headed back to Reykjavík.

Once we were back in the city, we found it odd that there was no ice on the ground, having spent the better part of a day surrounded by the frozen water. Our feet also felt very light, with no crampons holding us down. Finally, our muscles were still sore from the hiking and climbing. It was a day we would not soon forget.

Dining at the inn that evening, we had quite the appetite. We tried *hangikjöt* (smoked lamb) and had the traditional Icelandic cheesecake. A couple staying at the hotel joined us. I asked them if Iron Maiden was playing in town.

"Iron-who?" they responded as Sienna grinned.

This couple, Lulu and Roger, were in their 40's and visiting Iceland on his business trip. They hailed from Wales and were avid tennis players. Sienna told them of our glacier excursion, and they were fascinated but not sure they could handle the climbing.

Lulu then mentioned that they would be seeking the sometimes-elusive *aurora borealis* (or Northern Lights) that night.

"Do you want to come with?" she asked, in a proper British accent.

Meanwhile, in the next table, another couple, Jaime and Rick from Colorado, interrupted us and said they overheard we were talking about the aurora. The Coloradans were told by the hotel staff that it would be a clear night for viewing.

The six of us agreed to meet in an hour in search of this natural wonder.

From what Sienna and I had heard or read, the *aurora borealis* is majestic, appearing as huge curves and crescents of various colors interlaced with linear patterns in the vast sky. This visual spectacle results when protons and electrons from the sun (the *solar wind*) are drawn toward the North Pole by the earth's magnetic field and then collide with gas atoms in the upper atmosphere. The most common colors seen are red, green, blue, and purple.

The hotel staff added that the chance of feasting your eyes on the celestial marvel increases on clear nights away from the big city and the closer you near the Arctic Circle. This geographic line hugs the northern coast of

Iceland. With these useful facts in mind, our group headed north up the coast from Reykjavík.

After driving for about two hours, we had covered about 100 miles, halfway to the country's northern boundary. Still, none of us saw anything but stars and the moon in the clear expansive sky.

We all agreed to drive north for another hour. Alas, there was no aurora in sight. It was time to call it a night.

Most of the ladies in the bunch wanted to return to our warm hotel, but we men convinced two of them to take a detour to the famous Gullfoss waterfall east of the capital. The third lady, Lulu, eventually succumbed to the majority.

Meaning "Golden Falls" because the water looks golden in the sunlight, this immense natural phenomenon is Iceland's most famous waterfall and the most powerful in Europe. In the dark of night, we drove southeast until arriving at one of the car parks of the tourist site. We then hiked to the sound of the falling water.

On this moonlit night, the wide Hvítá River came into view. As we all walked further, the river seemed to disappear! Eventually, the answer to the mystery became crystal clear. The Hvítá had plummeted into a deep fissure, and we soon were able to see the giant Gullfoss waterfall.

The mighty Gullfoss sounded like Zeus was wielding his thunderbolt over and over again. The loud crashing of the water 110 feet down was deafening and awe-inspiring. As the six of us looked on speechless, a bluish hue dominated the enormous two-tiered waterfall. A true natural wonder.

We all recognized how small we were while standing next to the gigantic Gullfoss. But as the six of us left the "Golden Falls" area, we felt more energized and willing to tackle anything in our paths. In our drive back to Reykjavík, everyone expressed a sense of satisfaction with our road trip, almost forgetting about our unsuccessful search for the aurora.

Once back at the inn, the three couples gathered one last time and had some Viking Gold beer, Iceland's most popular. All of us agreed that the roar of the Gullfoss had become etched into our minds. And we talked into the wee hours about past adventures before exchanging addresses and saying goodbyes.

The next morning, Sienna and I packed and drove to Keflavík International Airport. We returned the dependable Kia rental and obtained our boarding passes. With time to spare, we meandered around the airport waiting for our flight home.

Both of us caught sight of an interesting display: aluminum sculptures of four standing life-size human figures, each facing one of the four cardinal points of the compass. Named *Directions*, this work of art by renowned Icelandic artist Steinunn Thórarinsdóttir symbolizes her keen observation that people's life paths carry them in various directions.

Whatever directions our life paths would take us, Sienna and I vowed to return to the Land of the North one day, if only to catch a sight of the *aurora borealis*. But the lasting transcendent image in my mind's eye still remains: standing on ice and seeing ice for miles around me atop the ice wall in Sólheimajökull.

Sólheimajökull glacier, Iceland

CHAPTER X:
Offshore

Blessed with at least 300 days of sunshine every year, the resort and tourist town of Santa Barbara, California, has been dubbed the "American Riviera." Lying about two hours up the coast from Los Angeles, it possesses a Mediterranean climate and a stretch of beautiful beaches.

I was the fortunate resident of this sun-soaked city for my internship year after medical school. And although the intern year may well be the most challenging in a young doctor's career, the weather and lifestyle in this Pacific paradise made that year manageable.

Leadbetter Beach is one of the most popular in the region, with surfing and sailing enjoyed by many. The campus of Santa Barbara City College lies right over this large crescent-shaped city beach. The long and narrow Shoreline Park also overlooks Leadbetter and offers fabulous views, picnic facilities, and a playground to this town's 90,000 residents and tourists alike.

On one of my few "golden weekends" of the intern year – meaning no hospital or patient responsibilities from Friday evening to about 6 a.m. Monday morning – my girlfriend Sienna came up with the idea of kayaking. Neither of us had ever ventured into this sport or activity, but we felt our physical fitness was good enough to navigate these human-powered watercrafts.

Canoes and kayaks have been around for as long as people have been propelling themselves along the water. Kayaks, which have evolved from the ancient skin-covered boats of the Inuit, are driven along the water with double-bladed paddles. By contrast, single-bladed paddles provide the thrust to move canoes (which developed from either dugout or birch bark covered boats of the North American Indian).

In general, the kayak is faster in the water but more unstable. But since it is more streamlined in shape and has a lower profile on the water compared to a canoe, the kayak is less affected by the wind. Moreover, the kayak is more maneuverable, meaning a higher fun factor.

We agreed that the kayak option was the way to go – if we could overcome the common perception that novice kayakers have been known to tip the boat over and have difficulty getting the boat upright again.

On Saturday morning, I looked outside and saw the sun and blue skies, with a mild breeze blowing on my face. Sienna came over and we drove to the kayak rental shop near Leadbetter Beach. After signing some waivers, we obtained our life vests. No wetsuits were required in this weather according to Danny, the sufficiently-tanned resident kayak expert.

I sported my dark blue long-sleeve rash guard and swim trunks, while Sienna was looking good in her kelly green one-piece swimsuit with overlying long-sleeve swim shirt and shorts. Both of us generously applied the SPF 30 sunscreen as we donned our sunglasses.

My kayak would be yellow and hers red. A safety video was shown to us, then Danny, who could be mistaken for a tanned Henry Winkler, gave us a brief kayaking lesson. Soon after, he helped us carry our boats along the beach to the water's edge.

First Sienna stepped into the cockpit of her vessel, followed by my entry into the yellow kayak. We were traveling lightly, so there was no need for the storage compartments in the kayaks.

A *spray skirt*, which fits around the waist and connects to the *coaming* (raised edge) of the cockpit, was optional and we declined.

In position and with paddle in hand, my girlfriend said she was ready, prompting Danny to push her boat off the beach. Less than a minute later, my kayak was thrust into the water.

Slowly at first, we used the double-bladed paddles to propel our vessels, stroking on one side and then the other. In no time, we picked up the pace and realized the speed capabilities of this watercraft. Eventually, this feeling of gliding along the water using just a paddle became quite invigorating.

Around us, there were others taking advantage of the pleasant weekend day, with sailboats and PWC's (personal watercrafts or Jet Skis or WaveRunners) as well as other kayaks in the vicinity. The weather had become cooler since the morning, but only a few scattered clouds were visible.

As we continued to go faster with each stroke, a friendly competition developed between my girlfriend and me. Soon, our boats were moving farther and farther from the beach. By my estimate, the distance to shore was now about a mile, give or take. Meanwhile, the water was becoming mildly rough, but we successfully maintained our kayaks steady in the upright position.

After paddling for about 15 more minutes, Sienna and I took a short break as our sleek boats slowed to a near stop a few feet away. We took photos of the now distant shore as well as the other watercrafts in our vicinity. Such a halcyon scene could not have been better scripted. But it may have been too perfect.

Seemingly out of nowhere, a gust of wind blew on our faces. Then another. The sun had suddenly disappeared behind gray clouds, and our kayaks were now rocking due to air blasts coming from different directions.

"Time to call it a day," yelled a mildly tense Sienna.

I concurred with a nod and pointed to the nearest shoreline, which by my estimate was only a mile and a half away. My girlfriend and I quickly began to paddle with a sense of urgency. As our boats turned to face the beach, we increased the tempo of our strokes and were making progress toward land. Our ride was considerably slowed, however, by the waves that were now over a foot high. To top it all, it began to drizzle.

An offshore wind, blowing from land out to sea, offered some resistance as we paddled to escape the incorrigible water around us. Sienna stopped for a short while due to fatigue, but I managed to get her moving again with a brief pep talk.

In our struggle to get to shore, the force of a large wave nearly turned my boat over. Meanwhile, Sienna was moving rather slowly in her vessel as water from all directions splashed on her body and caused her watercraft to rock side to side. It was a wonder we were still upright in our kayaks.

Alas, our best efforts notwithstanding, we fell victim to the fury of Mother Nature.

Almost simultaneously, both of our vessels, about ten feet apart at this point, were flung in different directions by blasts of wind and the resulting swells. My girlfriend was thrown out of her boat but managed to grab the side of her cockpit. I, on the other hand, was able to stay in the cockpit of my kayak, which was now on its side on the water surface.

Unable to right my boat, I recalled that my cell phone was in my swim trunks. To play it safe, I took the phone out of its waterproof case and decided to call the kayak shop. Fortunately,

Danny answered and asked me if the wind and precipitation had become problematic. After I described our situation, he asked where we were. All I could say was somewhere about a mile or two from shore and with some view of the houses at the Shoreline Park cliffs, which overlooked Leadbetter Beach.

With that, Danny instructed me to stay warm and keep my life jacket in place. He would call for help. As he said those words, my phone slipped out of my hand into the water. Still unsuccessful at righting my boat, I left the cockpit and held on.

Waves were breaking over our heads, but our sunglasses stayed on thanks to durable straps. The water had become mildly cold, and our bodies were only kept warm by our swimwear and life vests. I told Sienna to secure her life jacket, and both of us stayed afloat with relative ease.

As time passed, we began to feel the effects of the cool water. Something I learned a while ago suddenly came to mind: Stay warm by sharing body heat. Not seeing any rescue boat in the immediate area, I suggested to my girlfriend that we abandon one of the kayaks and stay together while grasping the other one.

Sienna's red kayak was now upside down, and she was unable to turn it over. She let it go, swam toward my boat, and took hold of my neck and torso. The waves around us were now almost two feet high, but we did not panic – at least on the outside.

With one hand on my kayak and the other hugging Sienna, I asked her to hold on tightly to the boat and me. After a few minutes, our bodies felt warmer. The current was apparently moving us toward the shore, but ever so slowly. On closer inspection, the water seemed to be pushing us more along the shore, that is, like a side current.

Our yellow kayak was still on its side, slowly filling up with water. I figured it would stay afloat more easily if we could remove that water. Once we were warm enough, Sienna and I worked together and finally got our remaining boat upright. In one of the storage hatches, she found a pitcher. Using this container, we slowly bailed out most of the water.

The surrounding waves, now over two feet high, were not backing down. We continued to hold on to the bright kayak at the edge of the cockpit, as both of us tried unsuccessfully to get Sienna, who weighed less than me, back into the cockpit.

As our efforts to get to safety continued, I found it difficult to imagine what it would have been like if only a single kayaker had been caught in our situation. With no one to talk to or grab hold of, a dreary attitude was likely to set in as minutes and maybe hours passed without rescue.

Meanwhile, our bodies were feeling colder in spite of our sharing of bodily warmth. I told my girlfriend that I had an idea. We draped our bodies over the *deck* (upper surface) of the kayak, mine in front of the cockpit and hers behind it to balance the boat. In this way, we minimized our exposure to the now cold water.

Sienna and I believed we were in reasonable physical shape but at the same time wondered how long our optimistic outlook would last. Also, we realized that it had been almost an hour since my call to Danny.

In an attempt to break the tension, I smirked, "Well, we did want an unforgettable weekend!"

She let out a nervous chuckle as swells continued to attack our faces and bodies and the light rain persisted.

The sound of her mild laughter was soon replaced by that of an engine. Like music to our ears, the roar of a motorized watercraft became perceptible. "United States Coast Guard" was emblazoned on the vehicle, and one of the uniformed men on board offered his assistance.

They got to work quickly. With ropes and fasteners, our boat was connected to theirs. In less than five minutes, Sienna and I were pulled into the Coast Guard vessel and blankets were wrapped around us. We then remembered how true warmth felt.

As we rode to shore in the USCG boat, I asked if the search and rescue personnel had been busy that day. Officer Drew, in charge of the vessel, said that his colleagues had already rescued five others (two kayakers, three sailors) that afternoon and more distress calls were coming in.

The strong air currents and prominent waves and mild rain persisted in surrounding the rescue vessel. One of Drew's fellow crewmembers told us that winds had reached gusts of up to 30 miles per hour in the last hour or so. Oddly, there had been no warning of such weather in the morning forecast that day.

My girlfriend and I were riding in a rescue boat or Special Purpose Craft (SPC) manned by three Coast Guardsmen. The Coast Guard is a branch of the U.S. Armed Forces that now operates under the Department of Homeland Security. Its responsibility for civilian safety in U.S. waters has a long tradition, dating back to its founding in 1790.

At last reaching the beach, Sienna and I conveyed our sincere gratitude to the capable Coast Guard crew. They then released the yellow kayak from the rescue response boat and said farewell. Paramedics were waiting onshore and covered us with more blankets, asking if we needed any medical attention.

I replied, "Other than a lost kayak and cell phone, we're good. Thanks for asking."

The medical personnel took our vital signs and performed brief examinations on the two of us. They were satisfied that we were physically and mentally intact.

Various onlookers on the sand patted us on our backs and expressed their relief that we were safe. They helped us carry our surviving kayak to the rental shop and Danny was there to meet us. He embraced Sienna and me and said he was glad to lay eyes on us.

"It's a good thing you had your cell phone," he expressed with a smile.

I decided not to tell him (or Sienna) that I almost did not make the call, thinking we could possibly get back to shore without any help. That hard-headed, Y-chromosome-related, invincible attitude was fortunately overcome by a more realistic, sound, and sensible voice in my head.

The rest of that Saturday would remain gray and gloomy. We went to my girlfriend's place to wash up before having a satisfying dinner at a local Mexican restaurant. Our waitress mentioned the mild storm and asked if we knew anyone who was in the water that day. The eyebrows of Sienna and me rose as we opted not to rehash our adventure.

My girlfriend said, "If someone needs saving out there, I'm sure the Coast Guard is up to the task."

I went back to work the following Monday without announcing the happenings to my colleagues. Over the years, Sienna and I have only told a select few about our potentially disastrous day off the coast of Santa Barbara. Superstitiously, in the past, we were hoping not to jinx ourselves.

Since that fateful day, I have continued to kayak on several occasions, always careful to secure my life vest and have a friend or friends come along. My cell phone is kept in my pocket in a waterproof case and I usually wear clothing that covers my arms and legs.

Dr. Hugh Fisher is an Olympic champion flatwater kayaker born in New Zealand, and he is featured as one of the admirable athlete-doctors in my first book. Like Fisher, I have been drawn to this challenging sport, only without his *über-competitive* aspirations.

The endurance needed to paddle the vessel as well as the symmetry of movements that incorporate most of the body are the sport's most appealing aspects to me. In fact, I have toyed with the idea of completing a *quadrathlon* one day. In this relatively new multi-discipline sporting event, which began in the Spanish island of Ibiza in the late 1980's, flatwater kayaking is added to the triathlon disciplines of running and cycling and swimming to test one's overall fitness even more.

On the more relaxed side, this sport of kayaking has been fascinating to me because of the grace with which the boat moves through the flatwater and the relative serenity of the water surrounding you. In such a setting, paddling such a vessel can be almost magical.

Saint Thomas, U.S. Virgin Islands

Epilogue

"How old would you be if you didn't know how old you were?" Such a question was posed by Satchel Paige, one of the hardest-throwing pitchers in baseball history. He also asserted, "Age is a case of mind over matter. If you don't mind, it don't matter." Some memorable quotes listed in the *Baseball Almanac* by the man who was 19th on the list of Baseball's 100 Greatest Players according to *The Sporting News* in 1998.

The live-in-the-moment attitude of Paige and his dismissal of Father Time served him well in his many sports achievements. Could this view of life enhance all of us as well?

In my first book, *Jock-Docs: World-Class Athletes Wearing White Coats*, I chronicled the lives of various indefatigable individuals who were diligent in their pursuit of well-defined goals. They exemplify one of the central themes of the current tome: *Carpe diem* or seize the day.

And in my estimation, it is difficult to seize the day without taking the bull by the horns and facing challenges head-on.

It may sound trite, but to take charge of each day is not just a saying – it is a mindset. Discipline and the pursuit of attainable ends must be groomed in a willing individual.

The U.S. Navy SEALs refer to this discipline in their motto: "The only easy day was yesterday." Since you survived yesterday, that was the easy part. Each new day presents another opportunity to adapt to new circumstances.

Theodore Roosevelt, the 26th President of the United States, embodies the spirit of this book. Despite growing up with asthma and experiencing the tragedy of his father's death when he was only 20, he became quite the Renaissance man: boxing at Harvard, authoring over 20 books, fighting with the Rough Riders in the Spanish-American War, and winning the Nobel Peace Prize during his presidency.

Usually intertwined with the aforementioned concepts of taking the bull by the horns and seizing the day is the sense of optimism. According to the Merriam-Webster dictionary, it is "an inclination to put the most favorable construction upon actions and events or to anticipate the best possible outcome." And many suspect that optimists enjoy many health benefits and tend to be happier overall.

The optimist maximizes his/her successes and minimizes personal failures, working at his/her shortcomings honestly. On a practical angle, we should be able to learn from any failure, using that knowledge as an important step to our next success.

No doubt, more challenges await all of us. But it is up to us to meet those challenges. And in this book of memoirs, I have strived to underscore the precepts of taking the bull by the horns, *carpe diem*, and optimism in various real-life adventures that have come my way. Hopefully, I have motivated you to apply the above concepts in your everyday life as well.

At the time of this book's printing, the blockbuster motion picture *Lincoln* was one of the clear favorites to win the Oscar for Best Picture. It is fitting that the primary subject of this biopic was unequivocally a man who took the bull by the horns, successfully ending slavery and preserving the Union.

I will give the all-important last word to the 16th United States President, Abraham Lincoln, the Great Emancipator and rated the best overall U.S. President in the Harris Poll of January 2012. Affectionately known as Honest Abe, he gave us these immortal words that ring true to this day:

"And in the end, it's not the years in your life that count. It's the life in your years."

Thanks

Any omissions are unintentional.

Vital to this book are numerous people in my life who have been instrumental in many ways. Their contributions and assistance and support have helped me in this my second foray into the literary world.

What makes writing all the more enjoyable and social are these various individuals who play important parts in the formulation of the final product. I have benefited greatly from those who have shared in my various adventures and travels. In addition, I wish to thank those who have advised me on the format of the book, including the cover and photographs used. Others have contributed their invaluable recollections of certain events described in these chapters. Some even took the time to painstakingly review and opine on some of my manuscript drafts. To all of the aforementioned individuals, this book was not possible without your kindness and insight. You should all take a bow:

Carly Lemond
Jean Bethenhait
Manny Aquitania
Ron Aquitania
Melanie Harlan
Gary Parido
Tory Lane
Aster Aquitania
Carla Adelman
Doug Levey, M.D.
Joyce Williams
Howard Bolotin
Jeff Bloom, M.D.
John Pierson
Boris Khamishon, M.D.
Ron Yamane, M.D.
Jeannette Ortuño
Eric Marks, M.D.

Photograph and Image Credits

All red and black bull illustrations are courtesy of iStockphoto.com

End of Prologue: Moebel-ideal.de/images

End of Chapter II: Official photograph, San Francisco Marathon

End of Chapter IV: Thecosmosphere.com

End of Chapter VI: Official photograph, Solana Beach Duathlon

Back cover: Official photograph, Steelman Sprint Triathlon Challenge

The remainder of the photographs and images are courtesy of the author.

About the Author

Dr. Ray Aquitania is a chemical engineering graduate of the University of California at Berkeley who went on to Chicago Medical School to become a physician. His neurology training was completed at the University of California at Irvine

Medical Center and the Veterans Administration Hospital in Long Beach. He has had an active private medical practice in Southern California, specializing in neurology. An athlete and an author, he revels in world and domestic travel.

CPSIA information can be obtained at www.ICGtesting.com
Printed in the USA
LVOW11s0250031114

411743LV00001B/67/P